MORE PRAISE FOR *MANAGING TO HAVE FUN*

"Matt Weinstein's *Managing to Have Fun* provides hands-on techniques for building a more creative and supportive work environment. He issues a loud reminder that our most valuable asset is our workforce, and that the value of this asset is either diminished or heightened depending upon the atmosphere created in the workplace. *Managing to Have Fun* shows how any leader can bring out the best in his or her people."
—Gordon Segal, president, Crate & Barrel

"If you're convinced life must be serious and work a drudge, read this book. It will lighten your load and add joy to your life. Weinstein is a brilliant jester who knows how to help people heal their lives."
—Larry Dossey, M.D., author of
Healing Words and *Recovering the Soul*

"Sure, we all believe work should be fun, but it's not so easy to do. In *Managing to Have Fun,* Matt Weinstein is letting us in on how to do it and how to enjoy ourselves in the process. Count me in."
—Jerry Greenfield, cofounder, Ben & Jerry's

"Matt Weinstein is the king of corporate funmanship, creating senseless acts of humor, random gestures of generosity, kindness, and delight that will help you understand the promise, irony, and absurdity of business more easily than a Model-T stuffed with consultants."
—Paul Hawken, author of *The Ecology of Commerce*

"For today's fast-paced and ever-changing work environment, *Managing to Have Fun* offers sound, practical examples that can really make a difference. If you are searching for ways to improve team performance and gain a distinct competitive advantage, you will find the answers in this remarkable book."

—Frank J. Elliott, general manager, western area IBM

"Managing to Have Fun is a book that you must buy—Matt Weinstein lets us in on the secret of why his own company is so tremendously successful. The philosophy is simple: a happy workforce is a productive and loyal workforce. The pages bubble and sparkle with wisdom—how to bring fun, joy, and an increased sense of self-worth into the lives of executives, managers and workers, so that stress is reduced, loyalty promoted, and output doubled. If your competitors put these ideas into practice and you don't, your company will lose out. And, incidentally, *Managing to Have Fun* is more than a business book—it outlines a philosophy for living that will also help to strengthen relationships with family and friends."

—Jane Goodall, Ph.D., C.B.E., author of *In the Shadow of Man*

"Fun is what sets Disneyland, Nordstrom, McDonald's, and Wal-Mart apart. The fifty-two practical gems in *Managing to Have Fun* show the way to a productive, joyful workplace."

—Sheldon Bowles, coauthor of *Raving Fans*

"Bravo! The Maestro of Play has given us fifty-two fabulous fun-filled ways to boost morale and design a healthier, more creative workplace. Read *Managing to Have Fun*—it is guaranteed to lift spirits and increase profits."

—Salli Rasberry, coauthor of *Living Your Life Out Loud: How to Unlock Your Creativity and Unleash Your Joy*

"What a concept—fun at work! Matt Weinstein has provided a real service to those who dread Mondays."
 —Richard A. Moran, author of
 Never Confuse a Memo with Reality

"I really enjoyed reading *Managing to Have Fun*—it's full of good, practical ideas. I think it would do a lot of managers a lot of good to practice even a few of them."
 —William C. Byham, author of *Zapp!* and *Heroz,* president
  and CEO, Development Dimensions International

"At a time when words like spirit, soul, and fun are rarely used in business, Matt Weinstein puts these concepts in their rightful place—at the core of any successful enterprise. This book is anything but 'business as usual'—it's the way business ought to be! I highly recommend *Managing to Have Fun* to management and nonmanagement employees alike."
 —Charles Garfield, author of *Peak Performers*

"*Managing to Have Fun* manages that rare combination of being lighthearted without being lightweight. It's full of eminently practical and nonembarrassing ways to reduce on-the-job grumpiness and to make your organization a place where it's okay to experience joy—including the true delight of a job well done."
 —Mark Gonzosky, commentator for the syndicated radio
  show *Marketplace* and partner, Hard@Work, Inc.

Managing
To
Have Fun

Matt Weinstein

Founder of Playfair, Inc.

Simon & Schuster

New York   London   Toronto   Sydney   Tokyo   Singapore

SIMON & SCHUSTER
Rockefeller Center
1230 Avenue of the Americas
New York, NY 10020

SIMON & SCHUSTER and colophon are registered trademarks
of Simon & Schuster Inc.

Designed by Irving Perkins Associates, Inc.

Manufactured in the United States of America

10 9 8 7 6 5 4 3 2 1

Library of Congress Cataloging-in-Publication Data
Weinstein, Matt.
    Managing to have fun : How fun at work can motivate your employees,
inspire your coworkers, boost your bottom line / Matt Weinstein.
        p.   cm.
    Includes index.
    1. Employee motivation.   2. Quality of work life.   3. Incentives in
industry.   I. Title.
HF5549.5.M63W42   1996
658.3'14—dc20   95-25916
                                                                    CIP

ISBN 0-684-81848-5

The author thanks the individuals and organizations who allowed their
stories to be told in this book, but who did not want their real names used.

To Geneen,
for talking to a cat, for taking me away to the island,
for opening my heart.

Contents

Introduction:
The Playfair Story

For twenty years the Playfair organization has been a kind of laboratory for the development of fun-centered management skills. Every year the twenty trainers on the Playfair staff facilitate experiential team-building lectures and seminars for more than four hundred clients, spanning the corporate alphabet from AT&T to Zenith Data Systems. What makes Playfair unique in the team-building field is that we have developed a technology that uses laughter, fun, and play to help organizations build successful teams. We teach our clients that the intentional use of fun on the job can help them improve employee morale, heighten productivity, create a more people-centered corporate culture, and, ultimately, increase profitability.

In this book, you will read about some of the innovative ways of bringing fun into the workplace that our clients have discovered. You will also read about Playfair's own unique corporate culture, of which play and celebration are an important component. "If you take yourself too seriously," reads our corporate motto, "there's an excellent chance you will wind up seriously ill!"

At Playfair, we want our prospective clients to know right from the beginning of our relationship that fun and play are an essential part of the way we do business. My business card, for example, looks like this:

Matt Weinstein
Emperor
2207 Oregon St. Berkeley, CA 94705 (510) 540–8768

In fact, my own title in the company isn't even my favorite. My favorite Playfair title is Fran Solomon's, which is "Senior Vice Empress." And while our business cards are fun, they also serve an important purpose in qualifying prospective clients. If I hand a prospective client my business card and he looks at me with a puzzled expression on his face, then I know that Playfair probably won't be a very good match for his organization. But more often than not, our positions of corporate royalty set a tone of playfulness to which clients respond. When I send out a business letter on my Emperor of Playfair stationery, I often receive a reply signed by the "Queen of Personnel," or "Your Obedient Serf," or "Special Assistant to the Lord of Finance." Whenever that happens, I know that we are going to enjoy a long and fruitful working relationship.

The cornerstone of the Playfair philosophy is that playfulness is a forgotten language that adults can easily relearn. Once we recall that feeling of jubilation that we once knew as chil-

dren, we can even make *work* fun. This idea has been so posi-
tively received by our audiences that we almost always get a
standing ovation at the end of our programs. After a while, we
began to incorporate this fact into our advertising, and for the
last ten years our lectures and presentations have come with an
unprecedented money-back guarantee: If we do not get a standing ovation at the end of the program, we will not take a fee
for our work!

This concept of a money-back guarantee was intended to
reassure prospective clients of the quality of our work. And
since no client has ever asked me for his or her money back, it
seems safe to say that this concept of fun at work has been
well received in the marketplace. Over the years, however, the
money-back guarantee has filled many clients with great delight,
as they give me a hard time about the possibility of withholding
my fee.

At a presentation I once gave to the Control Data Management Club, the executive who introduced me to the group said,
"Our agreement with the speaker this evening is that if you
don't give him a standing ovation at the end of his talk, we
don't have to pay him. Now, I don't need to remind you that
this division lost over $10 million last year, and every penny
counts! So, anything you can do to save the company a little
money tonight. . . ."

Then there was the talk I gave to the national sales staff of
Avis, shortly after it became an employee-owned company. The
vice president of sales introduced me by saying, "I want you to
know that we have an unusual agreement with our next speaker
—if he doesn't get a standing ovation at the end of his talk, we
don't have to pay his fee. Let me remind you that we all own
this company now—so if you stand up at the end of his talk,
part of his fee comes right out of *your* paycheck!"

The only time I really got nervous about getting paid was just before I was scheduled to address the American Public Transit Association. My talk was entitled "Putting Fun to Work: The Power of Humor in Business," and just about ten minutes before I was scheduled to go on, Tom Urban, vice president of the APTA, pulled me aside for a "private consultation."

"We're hoping to get a free talk out of you this morning," he told me, smiling.

Naturally, I protested. "You shouldn't really hope to get the talk for free, Tom, because that would mean my program bombed. Don't even joke about it," I cautioned him. "Be careful what you wish for, because sometimes you actually get it!"

"Oh, you don't have to bomb this morning for us to get our money back," Tom assured me. "Have you taken a look at the conference program booklet? "

"No," I replied, bewildered.

With a wicked grin, Tom whipped out a copy of the booklet from his briefcase and pointed to that morning's entry. Right below the description of my talk, Tom had included an urgent warning to the members of the audience: *"Please note: Due to a traumatic psychological injury incurred during his youth, Dr. Weinstein gets nervous and anxious if people in the audience clap loudly or stand abruptly at the end of his presentation. Please don't get carried away and frighten Matt. Help him out by remaining in your seats and applauding softly and graciously at the close of his presentation."*

I was stunned, and Tom could tell from the look of disbelief on my face. Fortunately, he cracked up almost immediately and admitted that this was a special edition of the program that he had printed up just for me. Thankfully, the real booklet did not contain any warnings about my "childhood psychological trauma," and the two of us shared a good laugh about the whole thing.

In my professional life, I take pride in the fact that, like Falstaff, I can be "not only witty in myself, but the cause that wit is in other men." In my line of work, I can't very well protest being the butt of my clients' jokes—at least they're trying to have some fun! Sharing a laugh together not only gives two people a chance to bond emotionally; as we shall see, it also can help them feel better physically.

THE HEALING POWER OF LAUGHTER AND PLAY

In our work at Playfair, we have found that the intentional use of fun at work can be a positive force in team building, in customer service, and in boosting employee morale and company loyalty. But just as significant is its impact on stress management and wellness on the job.

People have been saying for thousands of years that laughter is good medicine, but only in the last decade has there been actual medical and scientific research to document that laughter and play can have a beneficial effect on your physical health. Notice that during times of hearty laughter, your entire muscular system relaxes. Have you ever glanced at yourself in the mirror after you've been laughing really hard? Your arms are limp; you have a sort of glazed look in your eyes, and a contented smile on your face. . . . That is a description of the state we call relaxation. There is a direct correlation here: laughter equals relaxation. That is why you may have heard someone say, "I laughed so hard I nearly fell out of my chair." It's true —your muscles can get so relaxed that it may be difficult to summon the strength to keep your body upright. It's impossible to be laughing and tense at the same time. Something has got to give.

Ever since the publication of Norman Cousins's influential book *Anatomy of an Illness as Perceived by the Patient,* there has been renewed public interest in the healing powers of laughter and play. In his book, Cousins describes how prolonged laughter helped him recover from a debilitating disease of the nervous system. If stress and negative emotions can make us ill, Cousins reasons, why can't laughter, love, and positivity help us heal?

Cousins devoted many years to studying laughter and the mind-body connection. Cousins (among others) believed that endorphins, the body's natural painkillers, are produced during laughter. Endorphin release would account for the pain relief and the feeling of being naturally "high" that most people experience after a period of prolonged laughter. Although Cousins's contention—that endorphins are released during laughter—has never been conclusively proven, there is incontrovertible evidence that hearty laughter can affect cellular development. Dr. Lee Berk at Loma Linda University Medical Center in Loma Linda, California, has proven that spontaneous lymphocyte blastogenesis occurs during laughter and play, which means that during times of prolonged laughter, T cells, an important part of your immune system, are produced in much greater numbers.

When I work with doctors and nurses, I caution them that while they may be convinced of the healing powers of laughter and play, the concept may not be so easy to communicate to their patients. I tell them that they should go back to the hospital and say to their patients, "You're going to need to play more in order to hasten your recovery." And I tell them their patients will probably look at them in disbelief and say, "Play? I can't play now. Wait until I feel better!"

But that's not the way it works. *You don't play when you feel better. You feel better when you play!*

WHEN AN ORGANIZATION HAS FUN

It doesn't take long to recognize an organization that places a high priority on fun and play. Fifteen minutes before I was scheduled to give a talk to the Retail Division of Quaker Oats Convenience Foods, I stepped up to the podium to arrange the notes and props for my presentation. When I reached inside the lectern, I discovered a pair of disposable diapers with the Quaker Oats logo emblazoned across the front. I waved the Pampers aloft and asked, "Are these for me?" Jim DeVries, the director of human resources for the division, ran up to the stage, laughing, and explained, "The diapers were left over from the Quaker Oats Academy Awards presentation last night. I actually received an award myself for being one of the 'Best Re-Producers.' " The diapers had been awarded to all the executives who had become parents in the last year.

I presented my talk on "Building a Team" to all the employees of the Quaker Oats division at a two-day meeting held at a resort location in Galena, Illinois. The entire meeting was conceived as a reward and recognition event, because the division had surpassed its ambitious sales goals for the year. In my talk I encouraged the employees to celebrate even the smallest of their successes, to support each other as a team, and to incorporate fun and play into their everyday work lives, both in the good times and in the hard times as well.

The next speaker was Marc Schwimmer, the general manager of Aunt Jemima products. With his video image projected on a huge screen behind him, Marc began his talk on "The Consumer-Driven Operating Principle." For several minutes Marc explained to his audience why the Convenience Foods Retail Division should learn to pay even closer attention to the needs of its customers. Then he turned toward the screen and asked for the first slide.

"Uh, Marc, you didn't give us any slides," came a disembodied voice from the audiovisual crew.

"No slides?" Marc looked surprised. Then a wave of realization washed over his face. "Oh, I know where they are." He looked straight out at the audience and asked, "Bear with me a minute, will you?" Then he ran off the stage, dashed through the audience, and disappeared out the back door of the meeting room.

On the screen, the audience could see how the video camera followed Marc to the back of the meeting room and, in mock David Letterman fashion, continued following him even after the doors had closed behind him. The audience saw Marc's mad dash down a long flight of stairs, across the hallway, past the hotel swimming pool, and across the golf course. He finally reached his hotel room, ran over to the desk, and searched, without success, through mounds of papers. "Oh, no . . . I left them behind!" he moaned, and out the door again, back across the golf course, and into the woods.

Out of the woods, past a herd of cows, and onto the highway, Marc ran. Cars zoomed by him in both directions. He passed a green highway sign showing "Chicago 75 miles." . . . Soon another sign appeared, "Chicago 27 miles." . . . Marc dashed off the highway and zigzagged his way through the crowds of pedestrians lining the downtown Chicago streets.

At last, he found himself in front of the Quaker Tower building. He bypassed the elevators, and sprinted up the stairs to his office on the eighteenth floor. Mark then searched through huge piles of paper until at last he found the slides and held them triumphantly above his head. He reached into his desk drawer, pulled out a bottle of Aunt Jemima Maple Syrup, poured himself a capful, and downed it like a shot. Then he ran out of his office and into the waiting elevator . . .

(Meanwhile, back in the meeting room, the audience had been laughing and shouting and applauding Marc's misadventures on the Big Screen. When he threw back the shot of maple syrup, the whole room exploded in a full-throated cheer of approval, followed by an enormous wave of laughter.)

Holding the package of slides above his head, Marc sprinted out of the elevator, out the front door of the building, and back into the flow of traffic, dodging pedestrians left and right. The audience watched him move off the sidewalk and into the street, off the street and onto the highway, passing road signs at lightning speed: "Galena 73 miles." . . . "Galena 22 miles." . . . "Entering Galena Territories." After running through a cornfield, he emerged briefly, then disappeared again into another cornfield. Finally, he sailed through the golf course, past the clubhouse, and into the conference building.

Marc was running past the indoor swimming pool when he saw a "Slippery When Wet" sign, dodged around it, lost his balance, and plunged chest-deep into the pool. Holding the slides above his head to keep them dry, he pushed on through the water, emerged from the pool, and stumbled for the door. He headed down a long corridor, up a flight of stairs, and, at long last, was back outside the meeting room.

Marc received a thunderous standing ovation from the audience as he finally staggered through the back door of the meeting room, holding the slides triumphantly aloft. (His hair was wet and slicked down from his plunge in the pool, but his clothes, amazingly enough, were bone dry.) He returned to the podium and announced to the cheering throng, "You probably want to hear the end of this talk even less than I want to give it. So instead we're all going to head outdoors for the Quaker Oats Olympics!"

As the gleeful members of the audience left the meeting room, they each received one of ten different-colored Quaker Oats T-shirts, dividing them into ten teams. The teams faced off in Olympic-style events based on the different Quaker Oats product lines, like "The Long-Distance Aunt Jemima Maple Syrup Squirting Contest," "The Aunt Jemima Pancake Flinging Marathon," and "Bobbing for Hotdogs" in a gigantic vat of Beanie Weenie—brand franks and beans.

Participating in the Quaker Oats Olympics gave the employees a chance to play together, relax together, and relate to one another in a very different way. It gave them the opportunity to feel good about their success through a high-spirited, fun-filled celebration. Creating a corporate culture that nourishes fun at work can have immediate beneficial effects on the way your customers perceive your organization, because people like to do business with people who like doing business.

INTERNAL CUSTOMER SERVICE

There's nothing magical about it—if your employees are enjoying their jobs, if they are passionate about their work, it shows. People are going to want to do business with your company. And, conversely, if your employees don't like what they're doing or who they are working for, that shows, too.

Given the fact that there are often three or four vendors

who can do the same job for me, who can deliver the same product at the same time for the same price, I have a choice as to which company I am going to give my business to. Sure, I'm going to buy with my head, but I'm also going to buy with my gut. In making my choice I will ask myself, "Do I like you? Do I trust the people who work with you? How do I *feel* about dealing with your company?"

Are companies where the employees are having fun, where they are excited about coming to work, and where they are answering the phone like they're happy to be there going to have a competitive advantage? You bet they are—a tremendous advantage. Those companies leave their customers feeling good about dealing with them. And the intentional use of fun and play is the easiest way to create that kind of an enthusiastic work environment.

If you want your company to provide excellent customer service, you first have to provide that same kind of attention and appreciation to your internal customers—your own employees. You can't expect your employees to provide "service with a smile" if you don't give them something to smile about! The intentional use of fun and play as a management skill can help create the kind of a supportive work environment that produces excellent customer service. In a corporate culture where employees are rewarded, recognized, and given an opportunity to celebrate their successes, an attitude of pride in the organization is passed directly along to the external customer.

Managing to Have Fun has both short-term and long-term implications for your organization. By adding some fun and play to your management style, you can help create the kind of organization to which your employees will want to make a long-term commitment, and where turnover and burnout will be minimal. The intentional use of fun and play on the job can have an enormous impact on team building, stress management, customer service, and employee morale in your organization.

In the Playfair organization, we pride ourselves on the fact that there are a greater number of employees with ten or more years of service to the company than there are with five years or fewer. It's not that we don't hire new people (our staff has increased in size every year since Playfair's inception)—it's that the veteran employees rarely leave the company. We attribute our remarkably low attrition rate to the conscious emphasis we put on fun, play, and celebration within the organization. As we have discovered at Playfair, a company that plays is a company that works!

THE PHILOSOPHICAL ROOTS OF FUN AT WORK

The idea that laughter, play, and fun are an essential part of life is certainly not a concept that is new to our modern age. Throughout recorded history, many of the great philosophical and spiritual traditions have seen the value of fun in creating a balanced lifestyle.

When Plato posed the question, "What then is the right way to live?" his reply was, "Life should be lived as play."

The Book of Proverbs in the Bible tells us that, "A merry heart doeth good like medicine."

In the Jewish tradition, the Talmud says that we will be called to account for "all the permitted pleasures" we failed to enjoy during our lifetime. What a wonderful concept that is— that life is not just about pain and suffering, but that an essential part of our spiritual development is to enjoy ourselves whenever possible.

And in the Buddhist canon there is a recitation entitled "Evoking the Bodhisattva's Names" that has always moved me. It says, in part, "We vow to bring joy to one person in the morning, and to ease the pain of one person in the afternoon. We know that the happiness of others is our own happiness, and we vow to practice joy on the path of service."

Imagine if everyone in your organization took as their personal mission statement "to practice joy on the path of service." If everyone in your organization made it a part of their daily duties to bring a smile to the lips of one of their co-workers in the morning, and to listen with an open heart to the concerns of their customers every afternoon, by those simple acts alone you would have created the foundation for some truly astonishing team-building and customer service programs. If you can create an atmosphere of trust and support in your organization, where people can say in truth that "the happiness of others is our own happiness," then you will have created a sense of team where personal jealousies and office politics have far less meaning.

Is an office completely devoid of office politics and personal jealousies actually possible? Probably not. But it is a vision toward which the members of a company can move together. In the Playfair organization, we have embraced the ideal of "practicing joy on the path of service." We know there will inevitably be moments of tension and possibly even resentment among us. We know that we will sometimes cause each other aggravation and maybe pain. But that doesn't stop us from trying.

Once you begin incorporating fun into your work, you discover that the deeper purpose for doing so is to help create a genuine sense of job satisfaction for yourself as well as others. In order to feel satisfied with your job, you need to know that your work makes a difference in other people's lives: in the lives of the people who work with you every day, and in the lives of the customers who are touched by the products and services you produce. A sense of fun on the job can help you excel at both, as you practice joy on the path of service. Fun at work can help you find a sense of meaning in your everyday work life.

I like to believe that the Important Questions businesspeople will ask in the next century will not just be about productivity, quality, or reengineering. I hope one of the questions will be "Having fun?" Because laughter and play and fun on the job can help create a culture of caring and connection in the workplace that is just as important—if not more so—than productivity and profitability.

"Having fun?" is a powerful question, because it puts the primary value on the *people* in an organization. It is a revolutionary question to be posed in the world of business. And once we begin to ask this question of ourselves as well as of each other, then we can truly transform the way we live at work.

Chapter 1

The Four Principles
of Fun at Work

Why a Company That Plays Builds a Business That Works

Work is not supposed to be fun. That's why it's called *work*.

Work and Play are supposed to be opposites, like Love and War.

"Make love, not war."

"Quit playing around and get back to work!"

Just as love is sweet and war is hell, play is fun, and work is . . . *hard.*

Traditional business wisdom says that if you see someone having fun on the job, then that person is probably slacking off.

This time, traditional business wisdom is dead wrong.

By having fun on the job, perhaps an employee is expressing the joy of working in a job that is satisfying to her. Or perhaps she has found a healthy way to deal with the stress and pressure of a difficult assignment. Or maybe she is taking a momentary "fun break" from a difficult task, to which she will be able to return more alert and energized.

But if taking a fun break and wasting company time both look pretty much the same, how can you tell which is which? How do you know if you are looking at someone relieving stress, or if you are looking at someone who is just goofing off?

It's all a matter of perception. When you see your employees or coworkers having fun, you get an opportunity to encourage an atmosphere of excitement, support, and celebration on the job. Once you realize that "goofing off" is in the eye of the beholder, you can look at fun at work a little differently. Instead of suppressing fun at work, you can begin to nourish and cultivate it, because the expression of fun at work can be extraordinarily beneficial for the morale and productivity of your entire organization.

I am always amazed when people proudly proclaim, "I never mix business with pleasure." I want to reply, "What is wrong with you?" If you want to build a successful team at work, your management philosophy should be exactly the *opposite*—you should *always* mix business with pleasure. You should be constantly finding new ways to bring pleasure in business to yourself, your employees, and your customers!

For too many companies, building a team means creating a high-powered, smoothly functioning organization that has plenty of muscle, but not much heart. It is the absence of the human side of business that depletes employee morale, and contributes to job dissatisfaction and burnout. By adding an element of fun and celebration to a team-building program, you can take an important step toward humanizing your workplace, and creating a sense of heart and soul in your organization.

The Four Principles of Fun at Work

How do you establish a corporate culture that values celebration, appreciation, and the human side of business? There is no right or wrong way—every business is different. There are thousands of ways you can approach the transformation of your own particular workplace. How, then, do you begin? There are four basic principles that can help you begin to incorporate fun and play into your business life.

Principle 1: Think About the Specific People Involved

Bringing fun to the workplace does not happen in a void—it happens as a natural outgrowth of what is already occurring on the job. And not everyone likes to receive acknowledgment and praise in the same way. You have to ask yourself, Who are the people on your staff? What do they like to do for fun? How can you match their style of fun when they're not at work with the way you reward them on the job? The better you get to know the individuals in the organization, the more appropriate and the more effective you can be in using fun and play for reward, recognition, and revitalization.

Principle 2: Lead by Example

The people in your company look to management for clues about how they should act. If the managers don't loosen up, the employees are not going to loosen up either. There is a famous business axiom that says the three best ways to lead are by example, by example, and by example. There won't be any fun in your organization if you don't set an example by your own behavior. Every manager's leadership style is unique. Take some time to determine how comfortable you are with the idea of fun at work, and then lead based on what you have learned.

Principle 3: If *You're* Not Getting Personal Satisfaction from What You're Doing, It's Not Worth Doing

Don't kid yourself. You're not just doing this for your employees' benefit or to build a sense of team. You need this for yourself as well. When you give on the material level you receive on the emotional level. When you take time to celebrate your employees' successes, you reap the reward of feeling connected to the members of your team. We have all known successful managers who have built a thriving business, but who wake up each morning with a feeling of isolation, the feeling that it's lonely at the top. Bringing fun to work is not a one-way street: this is for your benefit, too. Developing a sense of connectedness to your employees is essential to your long-term emotional well-being.

Principle 4: Change Takes Time

Be patient. If change is going to be effective, it takes planning. And it takes time to sink in. A corporate culture doesn't change overnight from one in which seriousness and "professionalism" are rewarded to one in which fun and play are encouraged. Change is like a dimmer switch: darkness gradually turns to light in almost imperceptible increments, and a corporate culture that has devalued laughter and play metamorphoses into an organization in which fun and play are an everyday occurrence. Start by planning a number of small events that give the clear message that the company is learning to celebrate itself and to publicly appreciate its employees.

THE FOUR PRINCIPLES IN ACTION

These four principles have been instrumental to my work with executives who want to use fun and play to build a team. In the following case studies you will see these principles at work in a wide variety of industries. Once you understand the way these principles function in the everyday work world, you will be better able to visualize the best way to proceed in your own organization.

Principle 1: Think About the Specific People Involved

Sarah Fizer, a secretary in Philadelphia, told me, "I've been trapped in the same job for over seven years, and I've *hated* it almost the whole time. I'm the secretary for three different account executives, but my new boss has really changed things around for me. For one thing, he makes a point of coming by my workstation almost every day, regardless of whether he has anything for me to do or not, just to touch base and check in with me."

One day Sarah's new boss appeared at her workstation at nine o'clock in the morning and slapped a thirty-five-page memo down on her desk. "I need this corrected and back in my office by ten-thirty," he told her.

Sarah started working on the project immediately. On page 10, she found a little yellow Post-it note that read, "If you get this back to me in less than an hour, I will take you out to lunch on Thursday!" When she got to page 17, she found a miniature chocolate bar taped to the top of the page, with another little note saying "You're almost halfway through—eat this immediately!"

"He always does stuff like that and I laugh out loud every time I get one of his crazy notes," Sarah told me. "But do you know what made that first time really special? I knew that while he was composing his report, he was thinking about me, about my having to type it up for him. And he thought about how to make that fun for me. That he would actually think about me making my way through that long report when I wasn't even around—that was totally different from anything that's ever happened around here before."

Everyone at the office knew that Sarah loved to dance. She brought her dancing shoes to work with her every day— "I couldn't *wait* for the workday to be over, so I could go out dancing," she recalled. One day her new boss buzzed her into his office. Sarah walked in. He was sitting behind his desk, reading some notes. "Come in," he said to her without looking up from his notes, "and please close the door behind you."

As Sarah turned to close the door, her new boss leaped up from his chair and pushed a button on the tape recorder on top of his desk. Loud dance music filled the room. "He came out from behind his desk, took my hand, and started dancing around his office with me!" Sarah recalled in amazement. "He wasn't very good at it, but we danced around for one wild minute. We were both laughing and we were both really getting into it. Then he gave me a big smile as he walked back to his desk. He turned off the music and he said to me, 'That will be all—thank you.'"

Sarah smiled as she retold the story. "I walked out of there stunned! But every week now, almost without fail, he buzzes me into his office, we share one minute of wild dancing, and then he throws me out. Nobody knows about this except him and me. But it has totally changed the way I feel about coming to work!"

Laughter and play on the job are not an end in and of themselves. They are a doorway, an entrée into being more human with the people we work with. When two people share a laugh together, when they share some fun together, there is an unspoken communication between them that says, "I share your values. I am moved by the same things that move you. You and I are alike in some way." That is the purpose of laughter and play and fun on the job—to create a bridge from the isolated world of work to the everyday world of the rest of our lives.

Laughter and play are a powerful way of reaching out and making a connection with another person, because laughter and play are a common language that we all share. The language of shared laughter and play is a language we first learn as children. It is a language that can cut through the artificial hierarchies that are created on the job. It is a language that speaks simply and eloquently to the fundamental human similarity between any two people, regardless of their relative status in the workplace.

I included the story of the Dancing Secretary in a speech I gave to a trade association meeting of several hundred manufacturing executives. Near the end of my talk, I opened the floor to questions from the audience. A well-dressed man in his mid-forties leaped to his feet and started shouting loudly in my direction even before the microphone could be passed to him. "You know, all that sounds great when you talk about it in a speech, but in the real world it's just a load of crap!" he said forcefully. "It will never work. At least not with my people it won't."

I tried my best not to get defensive in the face of his verbal assault. "What is it about your particular workplace that makes you think it won't work?" I asked him cautiously.

"You say that 'people like to do business with people who *like* doing business.' Well, I like to do business—in fact, I *live* to do business. But fun has nothing to do with it at our company. The reason we're still in business is because I'm pushing my people to their limits. If I started thinking about fun and play, we'd never get anything done!"

The executive's name was Marshall Hall, he later told me, and he was the president of a company that designed and manufactured overstuffed furniture. As Marshall had begun to speak, he had slowly shifted his attention away from me and toward the other people in the audience. By this point he had turned his back on me completely, in order to address the audience more directly.

"I just can't do the kinds of things he's been talking about," he said to the group, with visible emotion. "If I started dancing with my secretary," he continued with obvious distaste, waving his hands in the air for emphasis, "my employees would think I had lost my mind!" It was evident that Marshall Hall knew how to work a crowd and that many people in the audience agreed with him. As he turned back to me for my reply, the audience gave him a loud, sustained burst of applause.

I explained to Marshall that I believed that with one playful gesture, Sarah's boss had reached across the artificial barrier that separates management from staff. With the humanity of that gesture, he had communicated to his secretary an essential message: "We are going to spend more time with each other than with our flesh-and-blood families. If we can't create a living, human relationship with each other at work, then we're wasting most of our waking lives!"

But Marshall Hall was right about not dancing with his own secretary. A scenario like that was possible only if there was a previous history of trust between them. Dancing with his secretary was probably not appropriate for him, and I told him so.

"You'd better believe it's not appropriate for me," said Marshall with a self-satisfied grin, turning again to his friends in the audience. "If I tried dancing with my secretary, I'd probably get sued for sexual harassment!" This remark earned him another round of enthusiastic applause.

"But you need to understand that these things don't happen in a vacuum," I explained to him. "The fact that this secretary liked to dance was well known within the company. She and her boss had already established a bond of trust, so there was no way his approach would be misinterpreted as sexual harassment. It was clearly an effort to reach out to her on *her* terms, and say, 'Let's be real people together. Let's do something together that I know that you like to do.'

"I'm not suggesting that you dance around the office with your secretary, if that's not appropriate for you. That's not the point of this story. The point is that if you want to make genuine personal contact with your own secretary, you have to consider what kinds of things your secretary likes to do when she's away from work. What's her idea of fun? How can you bridge the world of work and the rest of life?"

I could tell that Marshall was considering my question seriously. He looked at me for a few seconds, and then shook his head slowly from side to side. "I don't have a clue," he said softly.

That is the first principle of *Managing to Have Fun:* Think about the specific people involved. It's not enough to show up at work one morning with a new bag of tricks and dump them on the people in your office. Everyone has his or her own style of fun, his or her own limit as to what constitutes appropriate behavior. You need to respect the particular individuals involved.

If you can think about the individuals who report to you —or those who work around you—and learn as much as you can about them and what they enjoy, you will be better able to create fun experiences for them. This book is filled with hundreds of sample suggestions of fun-filled activities that you can adapt to your own particular situation. But for these suggestions to be effective and appropriate, you first need to think about the specific people involved.

Principle 2: Lead by Example

Marshall Hall approached me privately after my lecture about the Dancing Secretary, and we had a long conversation that led to many more talks over the next few months. Marshall clearly understood that he was in a unique position to make changes in his organization because he was the chief executive officer. He was the boss. But he was afraid that if he started implementing too many changes too quickly, he might have a rebellion on his hands—or at least a lot of confused workers.

Although he truly wanted to make some changes in the way he dealt with his people, Marshall felt that any sudden change in a playful direction would not be accepted by his employees. Marshall also expressed some doubt that he could still get the same productivity out of his employees if he began to lighten up around the workplace. He genuinely felt that his employees had already responded quite well to the present situation, which he described as "Everybody's fearful for their jobs. They know they have to produce, or else they're going to get fired. And if enough people get fired, then the whole company's going to go down the tubes."

His situation seemed hopeless, he said, and then suddenly, he brightened. "I have an idea," he suggested. "I have a really good human relations guy. I can have a talk with him and he can come up with something fun for my people to do. That way I can be the driving force behind it, but I don't have to be actually the one out front doing it all."

Marshall was wrong on this point and I told him so. "You can't just be the guy behind the scenes," I told him. "You have to be publicly associated with the change, or else it will never catch on. And it's going to take time. If people are afraid for their jobs right now, believe me, they're not going to think it's safe to start having fun at work unless you personally go out on a limb."

In an attempt to inspire Marshall to give it a try, I told him about Dr. Jeff Alexander, the founder of the Youthful Tooth dental office in Oakland, California. Dr. Alexander held a staff meeting in which all his employees agreed that communications needed to be tightened up around the office. It was apparent to everyone that too many messages were not being responded to, and too many details were falling between the cracks. The Youthful Tooth staff members agreed to institute a policy of jotting down notes to each other. The form they designed for even easier, more efficient communiqués had a number of boxes to check off:

— 1. message
— 2. problem/solution
— 3. response

The employees agreed to one underlying ground rule about sending and receiving notes at the Youthful Tooth: every time you received a message, you would write your response directly on the same piece of paper, check the response box, and hand it back to the sender or leave it in his or her mailbox. That way communications were kept as simple as possible. In addition, all the employees agreed that no one was allowed to complain about a problem unless he or she was willing to offer a possible solution. Dr. Alexander genuinely believed that the people who first notice a problem often come up with a possible solution to that problem as well. He wanted all his employees to know that their opinions were listened to and valued, and in this way the notes would be more than just a way to vent frustration—they would also be a positive force for change.

It seemed like a great system, and Dr. Alexander was very excited about it. He rushed the forms into production, handed out an ample supply to everyone in the office, and waited for some Big Changes to take place.

But there was a problem: no one wrote any messages. For the first few weeks, Dr. Alexander found he was the only one who ever used the system. And even worse, no one ever checked their mailboxes. So even when Dr. Alexander wrote a message, he rarely received a reply until it was too late.

Dr. Alexander decided that radical change was necessary. He stepped up the number of notes that he was issuing, and on every trip he made to the mailboxes, he would randomly leave $5 or some homemade chocolate chip cookies in someone's box. Then he would walk through the office blowing an old-fashioned train whistle he had received as a gift from a patient, calling out, "There's green in somebody's mailbox!" or "Time for a snack! Better check your mailbox!" At least that way he could get his employees to check their mailboxes occasionally, which was a good start.

Still, no one was writing things down except for Dr. Alexander. So he decided to take drastic measures: the following week he went on a conversation strike. When someone came up to him with a question, he would reply, "Memo me on that!"

"But Jeff," the person would inevitably complain, "you're not doing anything right now. You've got time to talk."

"Sure I'm doing something," Dr. Alexander would say, picking up an instrument and pretending to examine it. "I'm waiting for my messages!"

Soon people began to see that the only way they would get any kind of response from Dr. Alexander was to write their question down. And once people got into the habit of using the system, they began to send notes to one another as well. This system gave his managers an excellent overview of the problems and issues that needed handling in the office.

So where's the fun, you ask? If a problem shows up in a memo over and over again, Dr. Alexander and his managers have a ritual memo-burning ceremony when the problem is finally resolved. "The first time we held the ceremony," recalled Dr. Alexander ruefully, "we accidentally arranged ourselves right under a smoke detector. As soon as we set the memos on fire, we also set off the automatic sprinkler system and drenched everybody in the room!"

The second principle of fun at work is that you have to lead by example: you can't ask anyone to do anything that you are personally unwilling to do. In order to create a safe environment for fun at work, you as manager need to lead the way. You may need to do something a little out of the ordinary to get things started, like bake some cookies, hand out some money, go on a conversation strike, or start a ritual bonfire, like Dr. Alexander did. And even if your entire management team winds up drenched as a result of your efforts, it will all be worth it in the end. Dr. Steve Allen, Jr., once pointed out to me that if you look up the word *silly* in the dictionary, you'll see that it comes from the root "sælig," which means "prosperous, happy, blessed." When you lead by example, you may need to take some risks. You may even need to be silly in order to be successful.

Principle 3: If *You're* Not Getting Personal Satisfaction from What You're Doing, It's Not Worth Doing

A few weeks later, Marshall and I met for lunch to discuss some ideas for bringing fun into his workplace. The first thing Marshall could do, I suggested, was to give some appreciation to his employees for things that had been going right. "Have you been giving positive feedback to people who have been meeting their goals?" I asked him.

His reply amazed me. "Don't you think if I start complimenting them they'll slough off in their work?"

I asked him if he had ever been thanked or given praise for work that he had done. He replied, "Yes, of course I have." I then asked him: "How did you react? Did you say, 'Good, now I don't have to work anymore?' Or, did it make you want to work even harder?"

He grinned and admitted that praise from his supervisors had motivated him to work even harder because it had made him feel good.

I then suggested that he might begin by writing handwritten notes to some of his employees. I said, "Why not make a commitment to yourself to write ten notes a week for a month or two, notes that say thank you for a job well done. Just a simple note that says something like, 'Your extra work on this project has proved very valuable to us, and I really appreciate it.' "

But even that sounded difficult to him. "I'm not even sure I'd know it if I saw someone doing something right," he said hesitantly. "We have an enormous task ahead of us in getting the company back on its feet, and I want to fix it all right now. My sights are set so far ahead that I can't appreciate the small steps people are making in the meantime. If we're not at the end of the line yet, it feels to me as if we haven't accomplished anything much at all."

"Okay, forget about writing the notes for a while," I told him. "Maybe you can . . ."

"Hey, I just remembered one thing I've already been doing that's exactly what you've been talking about," Marshall interrupted. "One day I bought 125 birthday cards, one for every person in the factory, and I signed them all. My secretary sends them to their homes on their birthdays. That's a good start, isn't it?"

I wanted to encourage Marshall as much as I could, but before I could think of anything positive to say, I found myself shaking my head in disapproval. "Right idea, wrong way to do it," I said. "Remembering your employees' birthdays is an excellent idea, and one that could help your employees see that their work lives do not have to be completely separate from their personal lives. But mass producing birthday greetings will not do much good for you in your own struggle against creeping workaholism.

"You signed them all at once, and then you totally forgot about them until this moment," I pointed out to him. "In terms of your own need to get to know your employees, the birthday cards are a total loss. You're pretending that you're interested in them, but in fact you're much more interested in being efficient. Even though it may help company morale—although frankly, I'd be surprised if it did—it certainly won't help your *own* morale. And right now, that's just as big a problem for you."

"But it's better than nothing," he protested. "It's a good start anyway, isn't it?"

"I'm not so sure it is. Your employees may see the gesture as downright insincere. Suppose one of your workers gets a birthday card at her home, but then she sees you in person at the factory that very same day and you don't say a word. She realizes that you really have no idea that it's her birthday. Then the fact that you sent a birthday card is a meaningless gesture and you look like a phony.

"Receiving a birthday card from you could be important to your employees if it represented something more than just a token gesture. If it were a genuine expression of your caring for them, then they would probably also see that caring reflected in a lot of other ways. In addition, it's a missed opportunity for you. You don't come out of the experience feeling enlivened or any closer to your employees. In the end, it just doesn't work."

I told Marshall that he was not alone in this situation, that many managers I had worked with had done a similar thing. I shared with him what Michael Osterman, the president of Osterman API, had done at his company. It had become a tradition at Osterman API for Michael to have his secretary deliver a Mylar bouquet—an arrangement of Mylar balloons with an array of candy bars hanging down from them—on the anniversary of each employee's hiring date.

"My secretary made sure to write down each employee's

anniversary date in my appointment book," recounts Michael, "so if I ran into them during the course of the day, I would stop and congratulate them. But of course there were many days when I didn't run into them on their anniversary. So I realized that if I wanted to make these anniversary celebrations even more special, I ought to start delivering the bouquets myself!"

"Do you see what a difference it makes if the CEO personally participates in these celebrations?" I asked Marshall.

"Yes, of course I can see that," Marshall readily admitted. "There's just one thing I still don't understand . . ."

"What's that?"

"Where am I supposed to get all of those balloons?!"

Principle 4: Change Takes Time

Marshall told me that he used to be able to relax on the couch, watching the ballgame for hours on end. That was impossible for him now. He said he felt guilty if he didn't stay at work until seven or eight o'clock every night. "One of my best friends called me last week and he told me he had given up on me. He said, 'I called you Tuesday night to go out and you told me you were too busy. I called you Thursday night to go out and you weren't even home from work yet. You're hopeless, pal. You're a lost cause.' "

Marshall turned to me with a hurt look on his face and said, "I think he's right. I think I am a lost cause. If my friends from college could see me now, they wouldn't believe it. Back then I was the guy who always had the most fun."

"So what you're telling me is that at one time you used to be the kind of person who could kick back and be spontaneous? You were a guy who knew how to have fun, and obviously that guy would be the kind of CEO who wants his workers to have fun. You'd like to have the old Marshall back. Is that right?"

Marshall nodded slowly, wondering where I was heading with this.

"So how do you get the old Marshall back? Slowly, over time, you take a series of small steps back in the direction you came from. But since you have so many people looking up to you now, you need to move cautiously."

I understood that Marshall was afraid that if he started acting "crazy" in his office, his employees would lose respect for him. I explained that he was right in not wanting to do anything drastic, that the best way to implement change in his company—and in his personal life—was through small, incremental steps.

Marshall's management style reminded me of Roger Kerr, who is the president of Masterpiece Advertising in Kansas City, Missouri. Roger had attended a Playfair seminar and decided to put what he had learned into immediate practice. "I realized that I ran a very tight ship," said Roger, "and I almost never praised or rewarded my top managers for what they accomplished. So as soon as I got back to the office, I decided to give a $1,500 cash bonus to two of my top people."

Roger wrote the two managers' names on two large envelopes and filled each of the envelopes with cash. Roger realized that this unexpected reward would be most significant if he delivered it personally, accompanied by some words of praise for the hard work the two had done for the company, so he had his secretary summon the two managers to his office. Roger instructed her to tell them that he had something important to discuss with them.

Just before the two managers arrived, Roger got caught up in an urgent phone call that needed his immediate attention.

The managers were left waiting in his outer office for fifteen minutes. When Roger finally bounded out of his office, he found both of his top people slumped in their chairs, apprehensive and demoralized. It was only in retrospect that Roger realized what had happened.

"First they get an urgent summons to come to the president's office," he told me. "And then I keep them waiting. Then they see two envelopes on my secretary's desk with their names on them. All this from a guy who rules his company with an iron fist, who has never given them much appreciation before. What are they going to think—'Oh, Roger's probably called us in here to give us a nice bonus?' " Here he gave a wicked little laugh at his own expense. "With my reputation, that thought probably never even crossed their minds. They were slumped in their chairs because they thought I was going to hand them their pink slips. They thought they were going to be fired!"

Marshall nodded at Roger's dilemma. "That's exactly the kind of thing I'm afraid of," he chuckled. "I can just see myself trying something like that with the best of intentions, and then having the whole thing blow up in my face!"

"But not if you do it in small steps. As Roger discovered, you can't do it all at once. For any change in behavior to be effective, it has to be reinforced over time. What Roger learned will probably be true for you as well: sometimes it is easier to change your own attitude than it is to communicate that change to people who have worked with you for a long time. It's going to take long-term, repeated actions on your part to bring about even a subtle change in your business."

Every business has its own internal culture, its own unspoken rules and behavior that become instantly obvious to a new employee. No one has to tell him how to act; he immediately

picks up on the nonverbal clues that define the corporate culture. Suppose he tries to have some fun at work but gets a
disapproving look from his manager, or a nervous reaction from
his coworkers. He instinctively stops acting that way. He learns
how to blend in and "act like a professional."

I cautioned Marshall that any abrupt change in his behavior, no matter how well intentioned, would only cause suspicion and distrust among his employees. And with good reason:
suddenly the rules are changing, and no one knows why. For a
CEO or manager to change the rules takes time, because changing a corporate culture from the top down requires trust. And
developing trust is a function of time.

CHAPTER 2

One Small Act Can Make
a Big Difference

A TRIP TO THE MOVIES

I didn't hear from Marshall again for several weeks. Then, one morning, I found a letter from him waiting for me at my office. "I have thought about our conversation quite a bit since that afternoon," he wrote, "and I feel I've made a bit of progress. For instance, I brought in flowers for each of the women at work on Valentine's Day—though I think they may have been too shocked to appreciate them. I've also taken to keeping a nifty battery-powered space ray gun in my top desk drawer for certain situations.

"Anyway, I feel like I'm still expecting too much too soon from myself. Even though I have been passing out more words of praise, it doesn't feel comfortable yet. I'd like to keep in touch with you about this. My friend Rhonda told me about a group of managers she used to meet with for drinks every Friday after work. Their rule was that you couldn't talk about work at all. In fact, the first person who said anything that was in any way work-related picked up the group's tab for the entire night! That gave me an idea to try something with my people during our big move next month. I'll keep you posted."

I was excited by Marshall's letter and I wrote back to him immediately. Several weeks later he called to tell me that his company had moved into its new headquarters over the previous weekend. "All of my managers showed up to help with the move," he gleefully reported. "Of course, they knew they had to if they wanted to keep their jobs!" None of his employees got paid overtime for assisting with the move, but Marshall now understood the value of rewarding them for their extra effort. "At lunchtime on Monday I had pizza brought in for the whole warehouse crew. Then, after lunch, I rounded up the entire management team in the conference room. Once I had them all together I thanked them for all their hard work, and I told them that they deserved a much greater reward than I could possibly give them. I told them how much I appreciated all of them. Then I yelled, 'Field Trip!' and I piled them all into one of the company vans.

"We drove out to the CineDome, one of those multiplexes that features ten different movies. I bought popcorn for each of them, and let everyone choose the movie he or she wanted to see.

"People were grinning and carrying on like we were out doing something really special together. It wasn't the fact that we were at the movies . . . it's that we felt like a bunch of kids playing hookey from school. Out at the movies on company time! Of course, the truth is that they had put in more overtime in moving to our new headquarters than I could ever make up for with a dozen movies, but I know they really appreciated the gesture.

"Afterward, we met in a restaurant to have drinks and talk about the movies. I wanted to make sure that we all actually spent some time together talking—about the movies, about our lives away from the job, not just the usual work talk. So I used my friend Rhonda's idea. I proposed that we all agree that anybody who said anything about work had to put a dollar on the table—since, after all, this field trip was supposed to be an escape from the job. Of course, people forgot, and we had fun catching each other, and collecting the fines. And then we gave all those dollar bills to one of the guys, so he could pick up muffins and doughnuts for our morning management meeting the next day.

"What I'm learning is that I have to try really hard to make this fun thing a priority, just like anything else. There are always lots of things vying for my attention. But I know now that if I don't make fun a priority, it'll just get lost in the shuffle. I'm not willing to go back to the way things used to be, so I just have to take time out once in a while to say to myself, 'Okay, you're swamped with work, but now's the time to have a little fun.' It may sound forced to you, but I have to be disciplined about it, or it just won't work for me. It takes practice and persistence. Having fun can be hard work, I guess, just like anything else worth doing!"

Marshall is still the hardest-working person in his organization, putting in fifteen hours every day. But the next time I talked to him he had just taken his wife to a hockey game the night before. "I know it sounds crazy that I had to tear myself away from the office at 6:30 to go out on a date with my wife," he told me, "but I'm really glad I did it. I think I'm finally starting to get back to the real me. I know that it's going to take time, but I'm in this for the long run."

"What I predict," I told him, "is that more and more of your employees are going to stay with you for the long run, too. Once you create a business where your employees can actually enjoy themselves, you'll notice they'll enjoy their work more, too. You'll see a lot less turnover and burnout in your organization. And I think you'll discover you've got quite a few long-term companions on your journey back to profitability."

THE GOOD SAMARITAN STUDY

Can one simple act, like taking your management team out to the movies, make any difference in the work life of your organization? You bet it can. One playful, positive interaction at work can inspire the recipients to act in kind, creating a chain reaction of fun and celebration to be enjoyed by the rest of the employees in the organization.

I first learned about this ripple effect a few years ago when I went for a run through the streets of Berkeley with my friend Dale Larsen. Dale is a clinical psychologist, and although we had been friends for a long time, we had never gone running together before. After stretching, we began to run and had only gone a few blocks when I noticed that Dale reached into the pocket of his shorts, took out a handful of coins, and threw them over his shoulder.

The first couple of times this happened, I pretended not to notice. But after a while it began to drive me crazy—so finally I asked him, "Dale, what is the story with the money? Why are

you throwing coins into the street?" Dale laughed and proceeded to tell me about an amazing psychology experiment
nicknamed "The Good Samaritan Study."

In the study, researchers positioned themselves across from
a pay telephone and studied the people who made phone calls.
One of the first things they discovered was that almost everyone
who makes a call looks in the coin return after hanging up to
see if any coins happen to be there. The urge is irresistible: you
just *have* to look in the coin return to see if the machine has
mistakenly returned your money!

This behavior gave the researchers an idea. The next day,
they randomly put coins in the coin return slot, so that some of
the people who used the phone actually did discover money.
The researchers then hired a young woman to walk by the
phone at the exact moment that the subjects were hanging
it up. When the young woman walked by with her arms
full of books, she pretended to stumble and drop them on the
ground.

Astonishingly, the researchers observed that the people
who found money in the coin return were *four times as likely* to
stop and help the woman pick up her books than were the
people who found no money in the coin return. They con-
cluded that *when we feel good, we tend to do good,* which also
means that the helping impulse is transferable. In other words,
if you do something good for another person, he or she is much
more likely to do something nice for someone else, causing one
small gesture to result in a giant ripple effect.

That is why my friend Dale was throwing coins over his
shoulder as we ran through the streets of Berkeley—he was
hoping during the course of one afternoon to influence the
entire Bay Area to feel good and maybe even do good!

There is no telling how long the ripple effect from a simple, unexpected act of kindness can last. Darlene Olga, who works for IBM in Westchester, New York, remembers, "When I was eleven years old, I went on a camping trip with my family. We got a flat tire way out in the middle of nowhere. My father got all the tools out of the trunk, only to realize he didn't have the handle for his jack. There was no other way to fix the flat tire. We were stranded. About half an hour later a local with a truck noticed us, pulled over, and fixed the tire.

"After fixing the tire, the man said goodbye to all of us, and started to walk back toward his truck. My father ran after him and tried to give him some money. The man shook his head, and I heard him say to my father, 'I can't take any money for that.'

"My father said, 'Look, I was desperate. I really appreciate what you did for us. You saved our whole vacation. Take the money, please. I really want to pay you back.'

"Then the man said something to my father that I've never forgotten. 'You want to pay me back?' he said. 'Here's how you can pay me back. The next time you see somebody in trouble, go out of your way to help them.'

"I am thirty-seven years old," Darlene recalls, "and I think of that man all the time. Twenty-five years later, I still go out of my way to help strangers and to pay him back!"

ONCE A WEEK: FIFTY-TWO WAYS TO HAVE FUN ON THE JOB

It is possible for you to have that same kind of impact on the people you work with daily. Remember, if you reach out to other people with a playful gesture, they are likely to remember their interaction with you for a long time.

Since there always seems to be an unending amount of "serious" work to do, there is hardly any time left for play—especially in the workplace. In a high-pressure work environment, there just simply isn't enough time to do everything you need and want to do, and generating a sense of fun and play is, predictably, one of the first things to fall to the bottom of the "to-do" list. The only way to keep a sense of fun and play in your work life is to consciously choose to make it a priority.

When you make having fun at work a priority, you are not only making the decision to reach out to your coworkers in a playful, upbeat way, you are also treating fun as an essential component of your basic job description. That means that you need to evaluate yourself on how well you are contributing to the creation of a positive corporate culture around you, in addition to the usual stuff, like sales and productivity. Make a conscious choice to think about the last time you initiated something fun around the office. Ask yourself, "When was the last time I thought about the people around me, thought about how they are doing? What can I do in the next week to help bring a sense of fun, play, and celebration to the community of people with whom I work?"

If having fun at work is going to be a priority for you, then it is a reasonable goal to try to initiate something fun on the job at least once a week. Even devoting thirty minutes a week to this project is enough to make a difference. What follow, then, are fifty-two different strategies—one a week—for a year's worth of fun at work!

Of course, not all of these suggestions will be appropriate for your work environment. With each of these fifty-two ideas, take a look at the core concept and ask yourself, "How can I adapt this idea to fit my own particular situation? What is here that might work for me? How can I change it around to make it my own?"

Some of these strategies are suggestions for company-wide initiatives to be executed by senior-level management; others are examples of things that a single employee can undertake by himself. Some of these strategies require subtlety and secrecy on the part of the players; others may require open, enthusiastic, public celebrations, with the full sanction and participation of top management. These fifty-two strategies have been tested on the job in a great variety of industries, and contain numerous suggestions for unexpected, fun-filled ways to create more reward, recognition, and celebration for the people you work with every day. Over the course of a year they can provide a springboard for powerful changes in the areas of team building, stress management, employee morale, customer service, and organizational productivity and profitability.

Have fun with them!

CHAPTER 3

Creating the
Environment for Fun

I remember a tremendous argument I had with my girlfriend way back when I was in graduate school. It was one of those explosive fights where I was so frustrated that I slammed the bedroom door behind me as I left. Then I slammed the bathroom door as I passed it. Then I walked over to the closet door and slammed it for good measure, and as I left the house I slammed the front door, too, extra hard.

I got into my car, revved up the engine, and then, just in case she was still listening, I slammed the car door as well. Then I pulled away from the curb, tires screeching. (I thought I was demonstrating my self-righteous anger with a show of strength; she probably thought I was demonstrating what a two-year-old's temper tantrum would look like if only a two-year-old knew how to slam doors and drive a car.)

As I drove down the road, I kept replaying our argument

again and again in my mind. I thought about how right I was and how wrong she was. Then I pounded my fist on the steering wheel. (I was *that* angry.) *Nothing* could get me out of that foul mood.

Then I saw this guy coming toward me on a motorcycle, dressed as . . . *Santa Claus.* I stared at the stupid red hat and the fake white beard flying in the wind, and I totally lost it. I started laughing uncontrollably. And when I finally caught my breath, I realized that I wasn't really laughing at Santa Claus at all—I was laughing at myself for acting like such a two-year-old.

The sight of Santa Claus on a motorcycle was a gift—a sign to lighten up, to stop sulking, to act like an adult. To remind me that very few things are ever as serious as they seem.

We all need to laugh and play during the good times, the times when things are going well for us. But we also need the healing power of laughter and play just as much (if not more so) in times of stress and pressure, and the physical surroundings of your office can influence you to take time out to celebrate your work and those you work with as often as possible. In times of stress and tension, something in your work environment can remind you to slow down, to take it easy. No doubt you've been through stressful times before—and you're bound to go through them again—but something as simple as posting your favorite cartoon on the water cooler is a good first step toward bringing the Santa Claus Effect to the office.

Charmaine Silverstein, Playfair's office manager, covered one entire wall of her office with action photos of the Playfair staff celebrating together in various locales over the last several years. People love to visit Charmaine's office and ask questions about the various scenes. "Wouldn't it be great if we could all have copies of these pictures!" remarked one Playfair staff member, admiring Charmaine's Wall of Fame. That remark was the inspiration for the Playfair Wall Calendar, which incorporated many of the photos from Charmaine's wall. This computer-generated calendar featured baby pictures of the entire staff, strategically placed on their birthdates, as well as famous dates in the company's history. Each month showcased portraits of staff members clowning around or featured a collage of special moments in company legend like "Playfair in the Seventies."

As the photos on the walls of Charmaine's office so elegantly demonstrate, your office walls are the most obvious place to begin transforming your work environment. Take advertising executive Susan Einstein Schwartz, for example. One day, Susan found herself staring at the blank wall of her office, waiting for a brainstorm. She picked up a pencil to doodle and noticed that it had the word "Hershey" (as in chocolate) written on its side. In a flash of creative inspiration, she taped the pencil to her office wall, and wrote under it, "Pencilvania."

Then she started searching through the rest of her pencil collection. In short order, she had mounted a pencil that was short and pointy ("Pithy Pencil"), a pencil to which she attached a piece of string as a hanging tail ("Prehensile Pencil"), and a ballpoint pen ("Fake Pencil"). She drew a face and put a pencil over the mouth ("Pencil-Thin Moustache"), then drew another face and put two pencils over the eyes ("Eyebrow Pencil"). She drew yet another face with a pencil coming out of the mouth ("Pencilectomy"), and a pill bottle containing some pencil shavings ("Pencilcillin").

Visitors to her office started bringing their own contributions, like a broken pencil ("Pencil Missing the Point"), a pencil with an eraser at both ends ("Pencil in Search of a Good Therapist"), a pencil resting on a window ledge ("Pen-sill"), and a

pencil hanging by a string loop ("Well-Hung Pencil"), until
her wall collection was filled with more than fifty different
creations.

"This is a deadline business, and copywriters need to produce on demand," says Susan. "Whenever I look up at my
pencil collection, I remind myself that inspiration can come
from just about anywhere, and that writing should be joyful,
not painful, no matter what kind of pressure we're under around
here."

Your version of the Santa Claus Effect needn't be prominently displayed on the wall, as long as it serves you when you
need it most. Playfair's Ritch Davidson discovered miniaturized
music makers called "Toity Tunes" that he placed inside the
toilet paper rolls in the office bathrooms. Whenever someone
pulls on the toilet paper, the Toity Tune plays "The Star Spangled Banner," or "Somewhere Over the Rainbow," or "When
the Saints Go Marching In."

"It's fun for me, and the other people in the office have
encouraged me to keep changing the tunes," says Ritch. "No
matter how many times the people in our office hear the Toity
Tunes, they always start smiling. The only problem," he con-
fides, "is that I've been told by guests who use the bathroom
that when they unexpectedly hear 'The Star Spangled Banner,'
they feel they ought to stand and salute!"

In a work world filled with seemingly endless pressures
and obligations, having fun on the job can often get lost in
the shuffle. If you make it a low priority, something to get to
after the "serious" work is done, you may never get to it at all.

Find something to remind you that it's time to initiate
some fun at work. Make it personal, something only you can
relate to, and hang it on your wall. In my office, I have a mirror
made from a tennis racket, the frame of which has been covered

with red feathers. Whenever I look up from my desk and catch a glimpse of my troubled face framed by those ridiculous red feathers, I'm reminded to relax, to have some fun. It's a sledge-hammer of a message to stop taking myself so seriously.

You, too, can find a way to help Santa Claus ride his motorcycle through your office every day of the year! Here are some suggestions.

Once a Week: Fifty-Two Ways to Have Fun on the Job

1 | POST BABY PICTURES

The Playfair staff once worked with an adventure travel company that asked all of its management-level employees to bring baby pictures of themselves into the office. The photos were then posted on the company bulletin board. Everyone had fun looking at the photos and laughing at each other, trying to figure out which baby grew up into which vice president. And when a visitor came to this particular office she would invari-ably be asked, "Hey, you want to see a naked photo of the president?"

For the staff of that company, the baby pictures meant much more than fun. They were saying something very im-portant about the nature of the organization. What they were really saying was, "Yes, we have positions of hierarchy and responsibility in this company and rules by which we relate to each other. But the bottom line is that everybody here started out as somebody's baby." A company with that kind of attitude is a company that can make great strides toward generating a sense of community at work.

If baby pictures aren't available, you can try another version of the same general concept. Charleton Memorial Hospital in Fall River, Massachusetts, asked its employees to bring in pictures of their pets. Everyone had a lot of laughs trying to guess which pet belonged to which owner, and in some cases it wasn't that difficult, since the two of them practically looked identical! One of the nurses brought in a picture of his thumb and forefinger squeezed together. He put it up on the bulletin board along with all the other pet pictures, and when puzzled colleagues asked him what the photo was all about, he replied, "That's a picture of my pet flea!"

Once a Week: Fifty-Two Ways to Have Fun on the Job

 ## CREATE A STRESS-FREE ZONE

The Brookstar corporation, an automotive supply firm in Troy, Michigan, set up a "Stress-Free Zone" in the hallway just outside its main conference room. At first, it consisted of just a hammock and an inflatable palm tree—to serve as a kind of retreat for creative thinking. Then came the "stress-reduction dummy," a large, inflatable punching bag with a sand-filled bottom. When decision making became impossible, "people would come running out of the conference room and beat the [sand] out of the dummy," reports sales manager Clyde Willetts.

3 | COLLECT SOUVENIRS FROM THE BATTLE

After getting tied up on an unexpected phone call, paper products salesman Sal Minetta was very late for an important client
meeting. Once he arrived at the building, he drove around the
block looking for a parking place. He drove around a second
time, and still—nothing.

Sal began to panic. He knew if he didn't act quickly, his
part of the presentation would be over even before he arrived.
He was starting to sweat.

Suddenly, he had an idea. He pulled into a NO PARKING
zone and leapt out of his car. He scribbled a quick note, put it
on the windshield, and ran in to his meeting. (Sal's note said,
"This is an extreme emergency. I swear I'll be back here in 15
minutes to move this car!")

Sal arrived at the meeting just as it began. And, as it progressed, he found himself staring at his watch, monitoring every
passing minute. Sal knew that his report was important to this
meeting. He strained to pay attention to everything that was
being said, while he waited for an appropriate time to leap in
and deliver his findings. But every few minutes his mind would
drift back to his car. No matter how hard he tried to concentrate
on what was being discussed, he was completely preoccupied
by the fate of his car, sitting in the NO PARKING zone, begging
to be towed away. When twelve minutes had elapsed and the
time for his report still had not come, Sal excused himself from
the meeting and dashed back outside.

It was too late. There was already a ticket placed under his note on the windshield wiper.

Sal angrily ripped the ticket from his windshield, and then he noticed that the police officer had written something in response to Sal's impassioned plea.

The note still read: "This is an extreme emergency. I swear I'll be back here in 15 minutes to move this car!"

But the policeman had added: "TAKE YOUR TIME!"

It was from an unlikely source, but it was a powerful, important lesson for him: it said slow down, take it easy, "TAKE YOUR TIME!"

Sal kept the note and framed it along with a photocopy of the parking ticket. It hangs on the wall of his office as a precious souvenir, a reminder that nothing is quite as urgent as it might seem.

Now that you're aware of it, you can probably find at least one "souvenir of the battle" this week to prominently display in your own office, to help remind you of the Santa Claus Effect. Remember, you're not going to do yourself or your organization any good by driving yourself into a frenzy every time you feel pressured. So, think about which part of the office needs that kind of a reminder the most. What part of your work environment causes the most tension for you? What would look good up on that wall?

LISTEN FOR THE MINDFULNESS BELL

One summer my wife Geneen and I attended a "mindfulness retreat" at Plum Village, a retreat center in southern France. The retreat was led by Thich Nhat Hanh, a Vietnamese Buddhist monk who was nominated for the Nobel Peace Prize by Martin Luther King. I knew that his teachings would help me learn how to relax the hectic pace of my life.

Thich Nhat Hanh taught mindfulness training, the theory of which is that most of us spend the better part of our lives worrying about the past or planning for the future, but we very rarely spend our time focused on the present moment. At this retreat Geneen and I learned how to slow down in order to pay attention to the details of the moment. The technique that amazed me the most was learning to listen to the ringing of the telephone as a "mindfulness bell."

Every time the telephone would ring, all 175 participants in the retreat would stop what we were doing, breathe in and out, and listen to the telephone ring three times. Then, after three rings, whoever was closest to the phone would pick it up.

The exercise was used to illustrate the idea that the frenzied pace of modern life only serves to prevent us from living in the present moment. If every time the telephone rings we leap up to answer the call, then we are living our lives off-center and out of balance. But, Thich Nhat Hanh told us, the ringing of the telephone can serve a much different purpose for us, if only we would let it.

Imagine that during the course of a typical day, you are distracted by regrets of the past and worries of the future. Imagine, then, that all of a sudden a loud gong sounds, jarring you out of your preoccupation and back into the present moment. That was the very purpose for which the telephone bell was used at Plum Village. Every time it rang and I looked around me and saw everyone stop what they were doing, breathe deeply, and smile, it made me smile, too. And it helped me appreciate that the present moment could indeed be a wonderful moment, if only I would let it.

When I returned from the retreat and went back to work, I was enthusiastic about the idea of bringing the mindfulness bell back with me. I soon realized, however, that there was no way we could let the telephone ring three times at the Playfair office before we answered it. If we did that too often, our clients would probably think we had gone out of business! But I loved the idea of using the ringing of the telephone as a reminder to myself to slow down and reflect, so I decided that whenever line four on the Playfair phone system rang, I would stop whatever I was doing, relax my mind, and listen to it ring until someone answered it. Since none of the calls on line four were ever for me, it was not distracting to listen to it ring and then resume my previous activities.

Every time I remembered to do this, I found myself smiling, and those few moments of reflection had a truly beneficial effect on my state of mind. I was feeling pretty proud of myself for having found a practical use for the mindfulness bell at work, until I talked to Arnie Kotler. Arnie, who is the publisher of Parallax Press in Albany, California, had also attended the retreat at Plum Village. When he returned home to his office, however, he went much further than I had with the concept of the mindfulness bell. For one month, Arnie and his staff were experimenting with a system where they let the phone ring twice before answering it. During that time they would stop all talking and activity.

Since things were usually quite frantic around the office, Arnie explained to his staff, this practice might make them better able to serve their customers. If they were more calm and collected, he reasoned, they would be better able to interact effectively with anyone who needed their attention—from incoming phone callers to the UPS delivery person.

I asked Michael Gardiner, the office manager at Parallax Press, what kind of instructions Arnie Kotler had given his staff when he first introduced the concept. "What exactly did he say to you? What did he tell you to do when the phone rang?" I asked Michael.

Michael gave me a surprised look. "What did he tell us to do?" he repeated. "Nothing at all. It wasn't that we had to learn to do anything when the phone rang. It was more that we had to learn to *not* do anything!"

If your business life is overwhelming, consider doing less with your time, not more. By doing less, you devote the time and thought essential to a job well done, in addition to creating a more productive, more nurturing work environment for yourself and your employees. And in a calm, nurturing environment, the quality of your service will improve. And so, of course, will the value of the overall service you provide to your clients.

Sometimes in business, learning how to *not* do something is the most difficult lesson of all.

5 | PAY FOR THE CAR BEHIND YOU

The Playfair organization is based in Berkeley, California, and to get to San Francisco from our office we have to drive across the Oakland Bay Bridge. Playfair has an unusual policy on bridge crossing: if an employee crosses the bridge on official business on company time Playfair will reimburse her for paying her own $1 toll, as well as for paying the $1 for the car behind her.

This extra dollar investment provides endless entertainment for the Playfair employees, as well as a wake-up call for the stranger in the next car. Both drivers come instantly alive, and an otherwise boring, everyday situation is suddenly made exciting. The recipient gets through the toll for free, and the Playfair employee immediately has to choose between driving along as though nothing unusual has happened, or slowing down and exchanging a meaningful glance with the other driver.

Sometimes the car behind will race ahead to catch up with the Playfair employee in order to see his benefactor close up. His expression, upon realizing that the driver of the Playfair car is a complete stranger, is priceless. And although the other driver may leave the encounter totally befuddled, he certainly is left with a great story to tell.

Playfair's Fran Solomon always has mixed feelings about paying the toll for a married couple behind her. She pays her toll, pays their toll, and then speeds away, as fast as she can, so they can't possibly catch up with her. But she always imagines that the same conversation takes place in the car behind her: "Mildred, I swear to you I never saw that woman before in my life!"

Our clients have responded very well to this idea, too. "Last night I came to a tollbooth," wrote Nancy Wellinghoff, the public relations specialist for the Hospice of Southwest Florida, "and I remembered what you said about paying for the person behind you. I was very excited about the prospect of my first 'toll deed' and quickly handed the attendant a double fare with a big smile on my face. I told him that I was paying for the next person also. He looked out of the booth with a puzzled expression on his face and said, 'But Lady, there's nobody back there!' "

Nancy, of course, changed the instruction to "the next person who drives up," and had a good laugh at herself. Because even with the best of intentions, you never know how things will turn out. I was once driving across the Bay Bridge, and as I approached the tollbooth, I looked in the rear-view mirror and saw two men in a white BMW pull in line behind me. "Perfect," I thought to myself, "Am I going to give these guys a thrill." So I said to the toll collector, "This dollar is for me, and this one is for the car behind me." I drove off, somewhat slowly, watching the scene play out in my rear-view mirror, only to see the toll collector take my $2, deposit one of them in her cash register, and pocket the other one! Then she calmly collected a dollar from the BMW and waved them on their way.

As the tollbooth receded farther and farther into the distance, my shock faded to laughter. I have always been a great proponent of giving unexpected tips to people who don't usually receive them: bank tellers, bus drivers, flight attendants when they clear the meal tray. It had never occurred to me, however, to leave a tip at the tollbooth. There was nothing to do but laugh, as I realized I had just tipped my first toll collector —against my will! I've subsequently tipped the toll collector many times, in many different cities, in memory of that first occasion.

Tom Urban, the vice president of the American Public Transit Association, had an original take on the whole tollbooth concept. Tom wrote me that, "I tried a variation of your idea of paying someone else's toll. I recently told a tollbooth collector that the guy behind me was paying for *me*. It didn't fly (probably needs more market research . . .)."

Once a Week: Fifty-Two Ways to Have Fun on the Job

6 | DO SOMETHING UNEXPECTED

In the real world of your workplace, "paying for the car behind you" translates into "doing something spontaneous, something out of the ordinary, for the benefit of the people you work with." When Howard Bronstein was the night supervisor for the High Point Residential Treatment Center, he would put his walkie-talkie inside a puppet and leave the puppet in a high-traffic location somewhere in the office. As his unsuspecting colleagues walked by the puppet, Howard would start a conversation with them from his outpost in the next room. "It really woke them up," says Howard. "Except for the few people who would walk right by and pretend that nothing was happening; most people would stop whatever they were doing to hang out and talk to the puppet for a while. This one guy thought the puppet was such a fun idea that he brought a few of his friends over to chat. Pretty soon a crowd gathered around, and the whole place came alive."

Howard eventually retired the talking puppet, but he brought the technique back to life one last time at Christmas . . . with a talking Christmas tree: "Hey, what's the matter, you walk right by here and don't even leave me any presents? Come back here!"

The laughter and play that usually accompany a spontaneous gesture like Howard Bronstein's are not the goal of such a gesture; rather, they are a pleasurable by-product. They are not an end in themselves but a means to an end, a way to begin to wake up the work environment.

That is one of the extraordinary benefits of acting spontaneously in your daily life—you can give the people you are working with, and yourself as well, a different perspective on the same old events. All of a sudden a common situation looks . . . well . . . *different* . . . from the way it usually looks, and everyone pays it greater attention.

Doing something spontaneous and unexpected will most definitely snap your employees or coworkers out of their everyday habitual behaviors, and provides you with the opportunity to meet them in unfamiliar territory—the present moment. By acting spontaneously, you give the people around you a rare gift—a reminder that life is fluid, not static; that this moment can be different from every other one that surrounds it; and that at this very moment life is a little mysterious, and yes, life is fun.

7   TRANSFORM A CUBICLE

Hector Jamello is a senior systems analyst in the information systems department of a large telecommunications firm. "The atmosphere around my office," reports Hector, "is pretty grim. Whenever there's any laughter in the hall, one of the senior managers comes running out of his office to quiet us down. All the managers can see is how to make short-term interventions, how to keep us in line, but they can't see any of the long-term consequences of what they're doing. They can't see that they're destroying morale, and that productivity throughout the organization is spiraling downward as a result of the way they're treating us.

"I talked to the vice president in charge of our division, and I told him that we had a real morale problem, and I could tell from his reaction that he didn't want to deal with it. His solution was to go up to some of the employees and say to them, 'How are you doing? Is everything going okay? Are you having any problems?' This being the first time he talks to any of these people in six months, what does he expect—that they're going to tell him the truth? Get real! Of course, they all said that everything was fine, that there were no problems at all, so now he feels justified in sticking his head back in the sand.

"It used to be that you could talk to our vice president, but he acts different ever since we got a new president for our division. The old president used to walk around and stop to talk to people—he even encouraged us to call him by his first name.

With our new president, if any of us even approaches him, you can see the revulsion in his face. He looks at you like 'A peon has dared to speak to me! And one of them even touched me —quick, I'd better run to the executive washroom and wash my hands!' "

When I asked Hector about the physical environment of his office, he laughed out loud and told me that he works in a room full of cubicles. "The young people in our company call them VFPs," he told me.

"VFPs?" I questioned.

"Yeah, veal-fattening pens! Not exactly the best environment for having any fun."

But it was through these very VFPs that Hector was able to lighten up his work environment creatively. For example, one night—the night before his friend Mary's birthday—Hector came into the office and turned her cubicle into a mock crime scene. He used police tape to cordon off the area, chalked an outline of the victim's body on the floor, and placed yellow tape across the entrance to her cubicle that said, "Crime Scene: Do Not Cross!" When Mary arrived at work the next morning, she had to tear through the tape in order to get into her space. There she found a "Wanted" poster fastened to the wall featuring a mug shot of her face. The "Wanted" poster detailed her numerous "fun crimes" against the company (including such felonies as holding unauthorized meetings in the hallway, taking too many trips to the water cooler, and forgetting her coworkers' birthdays).

Hector had hidden more than fifty birthday cards around Mary's work area. He taped cards to the bottom of her chair, pulled out books from her shelves and hid cards inside and behind them. He threw cards in the back of the file cabinet, slid them under her computer, and sneaked them into project folders. It took Mary the better part of a month to find almost all the cards, and later in the year, in the process of moving to another office, she found even more of the hidden cards. "There are still one or two she hasn't found yet," chuckles Hector. "But some day when she's going through some old files . . ."

All day long employees from other departments came by to look at the scene of the crime and to joke about it with Mary. The positive reaction he received inspired Hector to move on to even more elaborate constructions.

His friend Linda lived on a farm and was always talking about the cows that she considered her pets. She frequently wore T-shirts with cow motifs and her coffee cups featured a whole herd of cows. For her birthday, Hector turned her cubicle into a barn and stuck a huge inflatable cow in the doorway. He removed her chair and replaced it with a hay bale. For a present, he gave her an alarm clock that mooed like a cow. The rest of Linda's colleagues brought in bandanas and western wear and joined her for a group birthday portrait next to the smiling cow's head.

But Hector's masterpiece was inarguably the "shrine" he built for Marguerite, Queen of the Dial, named for a colleague who was famous for talking on the telephone for hours at a time. Out of cardboard, Hector built a four-sided pyramid over the top of her cubicle that extended over some other cubicles as well. Then he wallpapered Marguerite's walls with Egyptian "hieroglyphics" drawn onto large sheets of butcher paper.

Hector found an inflatable child's float that looked like a sarcophagus and laid it across Marguerite's desk. He put clay urns by the doorway and found some plastic toy telephones that he planted in her office as "treasures" to bring with her into the next life. He brought in an elaborate picnic and spread the banquet around her office, so she would have something to eat in the afterlife.

Hector then drew up a map of the pyramids that included some of the other cubicles next to Marguerite's. The map described Marguerite's tomb and some of the surrounding tombs, and identified Hector's own office as that of the Great Pyramid Builder. When Marguerite arrived at work in the morning, Hector dresssed her up in an Egyptian headdress and took her portrait as she surveyed the splendors of her kingdom.

Hector's other creations included a bombadier's cockpit, a tribute to Calvin and Hobbes, and a cruise ship (complete with anchor, smokestack, portholes, and an office full of tacky souvenirs) for a woman who had just returned from a Caribbean cruise. "I do all of this work as a gift, but I do it as much for myself as for the people whose birthdays we're celebrating," admits Hector. "My actual job at the company completely stifles my creativity. I'm a good systems analyst, and I like what I do, but designing these birthday environments gives me a way to express another side of my personality—the creative, theatrical side. I think of these projects months in advance and I keep a journal in which I jot down different ideas all the time. I work late the night before the person's birthday, getting everything ready, and when the unsuspecting person arrives for work the next morning . . . well, the look on his or her face makes every minute of it worthwhile."

8   TAKE A TRIP TO THE TOY STORE

Ric Grefe, director of policy and planning at the Corporation for Public Broadcasting, saw a giant stuffed banana in a toy store one day and thought to himself, "This would be a great gift for my two-year-old daughter." When he brought the banana home, however, he discovered that the oversized fruit terrified his little girl. So Ric brought the banana into work and left it in his office.

His coworkers found the banana pretty amusing and decided to dress it up in sun glasses, a hat, and a dangling cigarette. Soon the banana began to take on a symbolic significance, as it migrated from office to office. "If I missed a deadline," said Joan Katz, a research associate at CPB, "I knew the banana would be waiting for me in my chair the next morning. It became Ric's way of saying, 'Hey, you messed up, but no big deal. You can always be replaced by a banana!' "

If you don't have a young child, chances are it's been a while since you've been to a toy store. But if you want to build an environment that supports fun at work, now and again it's worth taking a trip to the toy store—not for your kids, but for your employees, your coworkers, or yourself. You're bound to find something cute or fun that will inspire you or help brighten someone's day.

Be practical: If you want to lure a mouse out of hiding in your home, what do you do? You put out some cheese.

And if you want to lure Santa out of hiding in your workplace, first you have to put out some toys.

 PROVIDE PHYSICAL FEEDBACK

Dan Minuta of Western Instructional Television found an original way to keep his colleagues on their toes during their weekly staff meeting. At the beginning of the meeting Dan arrived with a bucket of wet sponges and a bucket of flowers. He then handed one flower and one sponge to each of the attendees.

"During the course of this meeting, if someone says something that inspires you or touches you," Dan instructed his colleagues, "I want you to tell them about it, and to throw them your flower. If, however, they say something that you find offensive, or detrimental to the best interests of the company, then you are obligated to fling a wet sponge in their direction."

Not only did this method provide a fun-filled way to give instant feedback, but it also gave each person in the room a chance to see where he or she stood in relation to the other attendees on any given issue. One time, Dan recounts, he threw a sponge at someone who he felt was making an inappropriate suggestion. Much to his surprise, Dan soon found he was the only one in the room who thought so—because everyone else immediately began pelting Dan with their sponges!

10 | DRESS AS A METAPHOR

I once had the opportunity to attend an upper-level management meeting in Phoenix in the middle of the summer. In spite of the fact that we had the air conditioning cranked up to high, it was gradually getting hotter and hotter in the room. When we called the hotel for help, we were informed that the air-conditioning system in the conference room had failed and that it would take several hours to repair.

Rather than move to another, smaller room, we decided to stay put. Soon all the men in the room had loosened their ties and both the men and the women had removed their jackets. As one of the vice presidents took his jacket off, I caught a glimpse of the brilliant reds and purples that lined the inside of his coat. When I asked him about this later, he showed me the inside of his jacket, which was covered with brightly colored stars, comets, and galactic explosions.

"My suit is my uniform," he told me, "so I buy expensive pinstriped suits. And that's how the world sees me. But inside, on the side that faces me, I put the wildest fabrics I can find. That's the real me."

Barbara Potts, a microvirologist who studies border disease in sheep, told me a similar story. In order to check on the progress of the disease, she was constantly working with the sheep in animal pens and had to wear heavy boots and a protective coverall. But underneath, she told me, she sometimes wore her sexiest teddy, "So I can remember that there's more to my life than wrestling with sheep!"

Bob Cleveland, president of one of the largest Caterpillar Tractor distributorships in the United States, is another executive who has had to convince his tailor to put paisley linings in his formal business suits. But Bob, whose company has five hundred employees and six different unions, also likes to have some fun selecting his outer garments.

"Whenever we have a big union negotiation coming up," he says, "I come to work that day subtly dressed in black and blue—because I know I'm going to get beat up on all day long! It's my own little private joke and it helps keep me calm when things get hairy with the unions."

The next time you are preparing yourself for a tension-filled meeting with your supervisor or an important meeting with a major client, wear something that will bring a smile to your face—like boxers with red hearts all over them, or a lacy bra. It will be your secret little reminder that things are almost never as serious as they seem.

PUT TOGETHER A GRAB BAG OF UNUSUAL OFFICE DECOR: UGLY TIES, INVISIBLE PETS, PUNCHING BAGS, AND MORE

Tired of looking at the same old office space? Here is a grab bag of ideas that four creative managers used to spice up their offices.

When Larry Sullivan was promoted from staff instructor to consultant in the Quality Assurance Department at Porterville Developmental Center in Porterville, California, his new duties demanded that he wear a tie. His fellow instructors held a farewell party for him, at which they each presented him with one of the ugliest, silliest, or most unusual ties they could find.

Larry proudly displays his tie collection in his new office. He reports that every now and then someone will come into his office, walk over to his tie rack, and add a really hideous one to the collection. "Sometimes when I'm having a difficult day," reports Larry, "I'll change out of my normal tie and put on one of my outrageous ones. I'm instantly reminded of the support and good times from my farewell party. Besides which, in the next half hour, someone will invariably insult me and my tie, and give me a good laugh!"

Ron Hoffman, a pharmacist in Los Angeles, found a unique way to schedule breaks into his everyday work routine. Ron has an "invisible goldfish" tank in his store, next to which he posts daily feeding times for his nonexistent pets. At feeding time he invariably draws a high-spirited crowd of customers and employees from other parts of the store who come to witness the invisible feeding frenzy. (It takes a little imagination, but for them it works.)

Linda Koliber of Chrysler Motors found "a low-tech answer to a high-tech stress problem." Linda put an inflatable punching bag in her office and soon had a steady stream of visitors who wanted to take out their frustrations on it. "Sometimes the security people will walk into my office," says Linda, "head right for the punching bag, thump it around wildly, head back for the door, and all they'll say to me is 'thanks' on their way out."

Linda Sims, associate hospital director at Ochsner Foundation Hospital in New Orleans, has a gumball machine in her office for her visitors. She keeps a pile of pennies next to the machine, so the treat is free to anyone who wants one. "Most important," reports Linda, "it gives anybody who needs it a good excuse to drop in on the boss and have a little informal chat."

CHAPTER 4

Think Small: Going It Alone

The best situation in which to introduce fun and play into your work environment is with the full cooperation of upper management. But what if you are going it alone? What if you don't have the support of upper management, or if you are not even a manager yourself? Can you still influence others? Can you still make a difference? Can you still have fun at work? You bet you can.

Chris Wells works in the personnel office of the Burlington, Iowa, Community School District. When you walk into the office building, Chris is the first person you see. "When I started in this position four years ago," she recalls, "the culture was stuffy and uptight. I was concerned that I wouldn't fit in with the other people in the office: the women wore traditional, flesh-colored pantyhose and very professional dresses (no pants, never pants!); the men wore suits, jackets, and dull, boring ties. I was always the black tights and weird shoes type; I wear dresses, too, but I also like to wear pants and knickers. I also haven't worn nylons since my wedding fourteen years ago (and I only did so then because it made my mother happy!).

"The relations between the administration and the employees of the district had been somewhat strained for some time. Since I was the one who saw the brunt of the employees' anger and frustration, I decided to wear a different set of 'head boppers' every day." (For those of you whose receptionist doesn't don them daily, head boppers are made up of a skinny headband and two eight-inch springs, attached to which are a pair of holiday/everyday things: pumpkins that flash, bunny heads, glittery hearts, fancy shamrocks, basketballs, footballs, anything you can possibly think of.) "I used to wear a different pair of head boppers for each holiday," said Chris. "My favorites were fuzzy antlers at Christmas, white bunny ears at Easter, and the all-occasion Dino (of Flintstone fame) for any day I needed a pick-me-up.

"Needless to say, there was not one person who came into the administration building who did not smile, giggle, or outright guffaw when they saw me sitting at my desk, working at my computer, wearing these silly antenna-like things on my head."

Unfortunately, there *was* one relatively significant person who did not smile when he saw Chris's extensive collection of head boppers—her supervisor. "My supervisor told me at my last evaluation, 'If you've got time to laugh, you're not working hard enough,' " recounts Chris. "He told me that I didn't understand the importance of my position at the office, that I didn't respect the fact that, being the first face anyone sees, I am responsible for setting a 'good example.' So I took the hint and quit wearing my head boppers. But everyone else, from the president of the Board of Education, to the parents, to the salespeople that come into our building—everyone else said how sorry they were not to see something funny on my head. They told me that seeing me and joking with me about my headpiece always brightened their day."

Although Chris has abandoned her head boppers, she has not abandoned her mission to lighten up the atmosphere at her workplace. "I believe that when you laugh you feel better, you are more productive, others around you are more productive, you're not absent as much, and you're just a much nicer person to yourself and other people," she says. And Chris was not easily discouraged; on the night preceding the last day of work before spring break, she came into the office with her two sons and hid six bags of chocolate eggs all over the building—in drawers, in paper clip holders, in telephone cradles, in every open space they could find. "I had given each coworker a colorful invitation to the 'First Annual Easter Egg Hunt' the day before. When they started arriving for work on Wednesday morning, they acted like a bunch of little kids, scurrying around, looking for eggs all over the building. There were also two 'special' eggs hidden, and anyone who found those got to pick a special prize —one prize was a big, chocolate Garfield, and the other was a giant-size Hershey kiss.

"The hunt was a total success—everyone had a magnificent time. I'm just sorry it took me three years to do it. One of my coworkers had a bouquet of flowers delivered to me that day to thank me for taking the time to orchestrate such a fun activity. We work under a lot of stress and tension, like most people do, and we really needed an opportunity to be silly and childlike."

Can one person, working in isolation, in the face of a supervisor who is hostile to the idea of fun at work, make a difference in the corporate culture of her organization? Witness the impact that Chris Wells has had over time on the other employees in her office: "Since I began working here, the men in the office have started wearing colored socks and ties that feature cartoon characters or play holiday music. The women are wearing tasteful walking shorts, stirrup pants, and cool, flowery cotton dresses in the summer. Sure, they still wear their navy suits with conservative ties or professional dresses when the occasion calls for it, but when they don't have a big meeting, they now feel like it's okay to express their real personalities and personal tastes. I don't take all the credit for this remarkable turnaround, but people seem to be in better moods in this relaxed and comfortable atmosphere. We still conduct all of our business in an efficient and professional manner, but now everyone seems like a 'real' person, not just a cut-out employee."

It's not the easiest way to bring fun to work but, as Chris Wells demonstrated so effectively, one person *can* go it alone. Obviously, you need to proceed with caution. If you have a supervisor who does not take kindly to your "guerrilla playfare" antics at work, who resists your efforts to reeducate others about the value of fun at work, then don't push your luck. Remember, change takes time. Move slowly and subtly, and it will happen. Of course, if work gets too oppressive, it may soon be time to look for another job. Just make sure you don't get yourself fired in the name of having fun! You want your search for new employment to happen on your timetable, not on your supervisor's.

But if you can give the reeducation process some time, you may be surprised by the results. As Chris Wells discovered, other people will follow your example, and soon it won't be a solitary effort anymore.

12 GIVE ANONYMOUS AND UNEXPECTED APPRECIATION

There are many organizations where positive feedback is in scarce supply. This plaintive lament from a Fortune 100 company executive saddened me greatly when I heard it, but it sounds all too familiar: "At the office Christmas party my boss got really drunk. Then he came up to me and put his arm around me and said, 'I love ya, fella. Don't worry about anything. I'm going to take care of you. I'm going to look out for you.' Then, on Monday morning, he acted like he didn't even remember my name."

Even in the best of situations, hardly anyone ever gets enough positive feedback. The antidote is to take every possible opportunity to catch somebody doing something right—and tell him about it. Don't wait for the sales manager to notice that a sales associate is doing something well—if you notice that she is doing a good job, go out of your way to let her know that *you* appreciate her. If giving compliments directly does not come easily to you, a good way to practice is by writing an anonymous note of praise to someone you don't directly supervise, complimenting him or her on a job well done.

Don Erickson, coordinator of instructional technology for the Oregon Department of Education, invented a character for himself that he calls "The Stroker." The Stroker leaves anonymous notes ("positive strokes") for people who are doing things worth praising around the office. Don even leaves some notes to himself from The Stroker, to divert suspicion.

When a new employee named Clarissa joined Don's department, he put a note on her desk that said, "Welcome Clarissa, we're happy you're joining us." He signed it with the stylized "S" that is The Stroker's trademark symbol. Don was delighted to see that Clarissa posted The Stroker's note over her desk and kept it there for her first two months on the job.

Karen Kolberg, a longtime member of the Playfair staff, always uses the drive-through window at her bank on payday. When she puts her paycheck and deposit slip into the deposit cylinder she always includes a piece of candy as well, as an unexpected treat for the teller at the other end of the long pneumatic tunnel.

Playfair's Fran Solomon rips out a page from her Far Side calendar and encloses it along with her check when she pays her monthly phone bill. "Somebody at the phone company has to be spending their whole day opening these envelopes," reasons Fran. "At least they know that one of their customers wants them to have a good laugh once in a while!"

Jeffrey Randall, another Playfair senior staff member, likes to treat the patrons in line immediately behind him when he goes to the movies. When Jeffrey buys popcorn for himself, sometimes he'll also buy it for the person in line behind him at the movie concession stand. One time he turned to the man behind him and said, "Say, you look like a nice guy. I'd like to buy you some popcorn?"

The man was immediately suspicious. "What do you mean?" he asked.

"Just that," said Jeffrey cheerily. "I'd like to buy you some popcorn. It would make me feel good."

"Well," said the man hesitantly, "okay, I guess."

"Hey, wait a minute!" said the man behind him. "What's the matter with me? Don't I look like a nice guy? Why don't you buy me some popcorn?"

This was more than Jeffrey had bargained for. His immediate reaction was, "Wait a minute. I'm going to wind up buying popcorn for everybody in this whole place!" But then he thought, "Well, why not?" So he said to the second man, "You're right. You probably *are* a nice guy. Okay, I'll buy you some popcorn, too."

"Oh, no," said the man, waving his hands in front of his face as if to push Jeffrey's offer away. "I was just kidding. You don't really have to buy me any popcorn."

"I know," said Jeffrey. "But now I really *want* to buy you some popcorn."

"Oh yeah?" said the stranger, pretending to be offended. "Well, if you buy me popcorn, I'm going to buy you a Coke."

"Oh yeah?" replied Jeffrey, with false animosity. "Then you'd better make it a LARGE Coke!"

So the three of them, laughing and joking, finally reached the head of the line, where the man behind the counter put an end to the entire discussion. "You guys are all nuts!" he told them. "I'm the assistant manager, and just for that I'm going to give you all popcorn and Cokes on the house!"

13 PLAY THE TELEPHONE KEYPAD

Yes, you too can learn to play "Happy Birthday" on the telephone keypad. When one of your customers or coworkers is celebrating a birthday, call her up and play her a keypad serenade! I usually only get as far as "4-4-5-4-9-8-Hap-py-birth-day-to-you," before the person on the other end of the line cracks up. So the truth is, I haven't ever had to play the *entire* song, but so far it's worked just fine.

Caution: If the birthday recipient is not at her desk and you get connected to phone mail, *do not* attempt to leave this song as a voice mail message. Through some quirk in its electronic brain, the voice mail system absolutely refuses to record this innocent message of birthday cheer. I found this out the hard way when I once tried to leave this message for a favorite client. Instead of hearing "4-4-5-4-9-8" as "Hap-py-birth-day-to-you," the voice mail hears "4-4-5-4-9-8" as "Search backward–Search backward–Delete old messages–Search backward–Archive this message–Change Remote Access code." Which in its language is the equivalent of some kind of an obscene phone call, so it refuses to have anything further to do with you and hangs up.

The problem with phone mail is that it just can't take a joke.

Once a Week: Fifty-Two Ways to Have Fun on the Job

14 DELIVER MIDNIGHT CHEESECAKE

The next time someone in your office is traveling and stays overnight on business, find out what hotel he is staying in. Call up room service at his hotel and have a piece of cheesecake delivered to his room—at midnight. Ask room service to include a little note with it that says, "I'm thinking of you tonight. Are you thinking of me?" And don't sign it! Let him have his little fantasies.

You can also send an unexpected edible delight to one of your coworkers who never goes away on business. Have a pizza delivered anonymously to that person's desk at the office in the middle of the workday. You can be as creative as you like, too. When Playfair trainer Jeffrey Randall had a surprise pizza delivered to coworker Nikki Jordan, he had the pizza parlor spell out her name in mushrooms on the top of the pie!

Once a Week: Fifty-Two Ways to Have Fun on the Job

15 ORGANIZE A PAPER AIRPLANE FLYING CONTEST

Kirt Womack works at the Thiokol factory in Utah, which makes the solid fuel rocket boosters for the space shuttle program. Like Chris Wells, Kirt is another person in a nonmanagement position who has brought organized fun to his workplace, in spite of opposition from his supervisor.

The first day of mild weather had finally arrived after a long, brutal Utah winter. Kirt and his coworkers had been feeling cooped up on the factory floor, so Kirt approached his foreman with a proposal: "Let's celebrate the official first day of spring next week by shutting down the line for one hour and giving the employees a chance to go outside and have a paper airplane flying contest!" (After all, they are in the aerospace industry.)

Kirt's foreman looked at him in disbelief. "There is no way," he informed Kirt, "we will shut down production for an hour to have a paper airplane flying contest."

So Kirt huddled with his team for a few minutes and came back to his supervisor with a revised proposition. If his shift produced 150 percent of their daily quota by two-thirty in the afternoon, he proposed, then the whole team could go outside for a paper airplane flying contest. The foreman reluctantly agreed to Kirt's proposal.

At one-thirty, Kirt's team was at 110 percent of quota, and by the time two-thirty rolled around they had hit 210 percent! Everyone from the floor went outside and celebrated the arrival of spring by flinging their paper airplanes to the wind.

Kirt walked up to his supervisor and gestured to his team, who were laughing and playing together in the sunshine. "So, what do you think now?" asked Kirt proudly.

"You want to know what I think?" replied his foreman. "I think that if you can produce this well with an hour off, imagine how much more you could get done if you actually worked that hard for the whole shift!"

Obviously, his foreman had completely missed the point of Kirt's intervention. The team had not produced so well that day *in spite* of the hour off; they had produced that well *because* of the hour off. But Kirt was not deterred. The next week he huddled with his team again, and again he returned to his supervisor with a new proposal. Together, they would set a future production goal for Kirt's shift, and if the goal was met or exceeded, Kirt could bring in a volleyball net and set it up on the factory floor for an hour on an agreed-upon date.

Kirt's team responded with record productivity, and the volleyball net was triumphantly set up. Kirt has coined a phrase for these rewards he dreams up for his team. He calls them "non-work-related team-building activities." When Kirt approached his foreman the next week and proposed that if his team again exceeded their quota his foreman would take them off-site to an ice-cream shop to eat their fill at the foreman's expense, the foreman enthusiastically agreed. It was clear to him by now that the days of the highest productivity at the factory were the days of Kirt's non-work-related team-building activities.

Kirt's team worked even harder to fulfill their quota because the idea for the reward came from within their own ranks, not from management. As a manager, challenge yourself to create the kind of environment where your employees are supported for coming up with innovative reward and recognition ideas of their own. But remember, you first need to model that kind of behavior yourself. The three best ways to create an environment where fun and play are rewarded are by example, by example, and by example.

And if you are a nonmanagement employee who is faced with a resistant supervisor, don't be afraid to link fun at work with increased productivity. Set a production goal for your team and propose an appropriate reward. The purpose of fun at work is not merely to increase your enjoyment of your job—it's to increase productivity as well. The best way to convince a reluctant supervisor that joy and celebration are an essential component of the everyday workday is to demonstrate their impact on the bottom line. Choose a reward that will leave your team refreshed, renewed, and excited about working together.

You know that there is a link between fun and productivity. Don't be afraid to prove it.

Once a Week: Fifty-Two Ways to Have Fun on the Job

---

16 LEND A BOUQUET OF FLOWERS

Carol Ann Fried, one of the leaders of Playfair Canada, invented the concept of the "Traveling Flower Bouquet" when she brought in a bouquet of flowers to work one day and, as she presented it to one of her coworkers, said, "I want you to keep this bouquet on your desk for the next half-hour. Then pass it on as a gift from you to someone else, and tell them to do the same thing!"

Part of the fun, says Carol Ann, is to see how long it takes for someone in the office to give the bouquet back to you, having no idea that you are the person who started the whole thing. You get to keep the flowers for a while, then pass them on and start the whole sequence all over again.

17 | MAKE BUSINESS TRIPS FUN

Although we all like to pretend that business travel is fun, it can often be a very stressful experience. Business trips are more often about "business" than about "trips." So how can you make a business trip more enjoyable? I usually load my flight bag with all the makings of an in-flight entertainment center: my laptop computer, my video walkman, a selection of video-cassettes, and a collection of books, newspapers, and magazines. Sometimes I like to talk to the person next to me and other times I just want to be left alone. The moment of truth usually occurs during the meal service, when my seatmate leans over and says, "You on a business trip?"

"Yes," I reply. Then the inevitable question follows: "What kind of business are you in?"

If I want to be left alone, I simply say, "I'm with the IRS." This immediately ends all further attempts at discussion by my seatmate.

But one of the most frustrating business travel situations is waiting at the airport for a connecting flight or for a flight that has been delayed. When I was first learning how to juggle, I thought of a way to put this downtime to good use. I packed my juggling balls in my carry-on bag, so I could practice while waiting in the flight lounge—it seemed like the perfect way to pass the time and improve my fledgling skills. The only problem was that the sight of multicolored juggling balls flashing through the air invariably attracted a crowd of bored passengers, all of whom assumed that I was putting on a performance for them. My pathetic attempts at learning the three-ball cascade were far from being a show, however—I would drop the balls as often as I would catch them—and my fellow passengers soon retired from the scene in disgust.

Their disillusionment did not stop the next group of new-comers from gathering shortly, however, and soon the whole scene was repeated all over again. I eventually decided that it was better for my own mental well-being to leave my juggling balls at home and take up a less daring airport hobby, like talking on the telephone.

One great advantage of being away on a business trip is that you often have some unexpected leisure time. The next time you are alone in a strange city with some time on your hands, practice being spontaneous. Terry Green, sales director for the Wichita Airport Hilton and Executive Conference Center, was sitting in his hotel room on a business trip when he decided to go for a walk around the local mall. "On my first pass through the mall, I noticed a booth where tickets to the Shrine Circus were being sold," Terry told me. "I thought about that story you told about paying for the person behind you at a toll. I decided to try my own variation.

"I walked up to the booth and gave the lady cash for a child's ticket. Then I told her to give the ticket to the next child who showed up at the booth. I have no idea who received the ticket, since I did not stick around to find out. But I do know that the lady selling the tickets had a hard time believing what I was doing. Before I left the booth, she must have thanked me half a dozen times. As I was walking off, she was talking to the other woman in the booth and pointing in my direction. I hope I brought a little laughter and fun to the family that received the ticket, but I know for sure that I gave the lady selling the tickets a little chuckle. And it made the trip to Topeka a lot more memorable for me."

18 | PLAN A SURPRISE PICNIC

Several years ago, as I was looking over my travel itinerary for a business trip from San Francisco to New Orleans, I noticed that I was scheduled for a long layover in the airport in Dallas, where I was supposed to change planes. So I called my friend Luke Barber, who is a philosophy professor at Richland College in Dallas. I said, "Luke, I'm going to have an hour-and-a-half layover at DFW airport. If you'll come out to the airport and meet my plane, I'll treat you to dinner."

Luke enthusiastically agreed, and I was excited by the prospect of getting to spend a little time with him. When the pilot announced that our flight would be delayed on the ground an extra few minutes in San Francisco because of air traffic control I paid no attention, but as those few minutes dragged on and on into an hour, I became more agitated and upset. Every minute that passed was one minute less that I would be able to spend with Luke.

The pilot promised to make up the lost time en route, but he wasn't able to make up much time after all, so the plane arrived in Dallas an hour late. That left me only half an hour, during which I still wanted to visit with Luke—but I also had to dash for my connecting flight. I knew at this point that our having dinner together was totally out of the question, since DFW Airport is so huge that half an hour is barely enough time to get from one plane to the next.

When I stepped off the plane, Luke was there, waiting for me.

"Hey, Luke," I said apologetically, "thanks for coming out to meet me. I hope you didn't have to wait here too long."

"Oh, no problem," he replied easily, "I called ahead and found out your plane was going to be late."

"Oh, good," I replied, distracted by the time pressure. "Look, I'm really sorry about dinner, but I'll owe you one next time. Come on, we'll find out where my next plane is leaving from, and we can walk over there together and talk a bit." I started walking away from the gate area.

Luke didn't budge. "I am very invested in having dinner with you," he said to me.

I looked back at him incredulously. "What are you talking about?" I laughed. "The only way you're going to have dinner with me tonight is if you buy a plane ticket to New Orleans!"

"We're having dinner," replied Luke with determination. "Believe me, I have this whole thing scoped out. Just follow me." He picked up one of my bags and carried it out through the security check. I followed him closely, silently protesting and growing more anxious with every passing moment. He started running down into the parking garage, and I started running along behind him, thinking to myself, "There is *no way* we are going to get into his car, drive to a restaurant, have dinner, and still get back in time for me to make my plane!"

But then I began talking myself down from my panic-stricken state. "Luke is one of your best friends in the world," I thought. "He knows what time your flight leaves. The guy is a master of stress-free behavior. (When I give lectures on stress management, I always tell stories about Luke.) He says he's got it scoped out! Trust him." For once in my adult life, I actually gave up control of the situation to someone else.

The two of us hustled down a short flight of stairs in the parking garage and walked rapidly along several rows of cars until we came to the place where Luke's car was parked. I immediately noticed that in the parking space next to his car, he had set up a folding table.

Luke pulled out his car keys and opened the trunk of his car. He reached in and pulled out a checkered picnic tablecloth, which he spread with a grand flourish over the table. Then he pulled two folding chairs out of the trunk of his car and set them up next to the table. He pulled out a bottle of champagne and a container of hors d'oeuvres. He set a candle in the center of the table and lit it. We popped the champagne and broke out the hors d'oeuvres.

There we were, sitting across the table from each other in the middle of a parking lot, toasting each other with champagne, grinning from ear to ear. Carbon monoxide fumes may have been swirling all around us, but we didn't care. Drivers in search of a parking place were annoyed at us for taking up the space, but once they took a closer look, many of them broke into astonished smiles.

With seven and a half minutes to go, we put everything back in the trunk of the car and ran for my plane. We got through the security check with no problem and arrived back at my old gate, American gate 23, with five minutes to spare. What Luke had *not* realized, however, was that my next flight was leaving from American gate 31, which was in the other terminal! There was no way I was going to get from terminal 2 to terminal 3 in time to make my plane.

I was starting to get hysterical. But Luke was ready for

anything—he flagged down an airport employee driving an electric cart and we jumped on the back. "Our plane is leaving from gate 31 in three minutes!" Luke told him. The driver was up to the challenge. He drove the cart like a Grand Prix racer, dodging and weaving around the pedestrians. We loudly applauded his every move. We were laughing. We were screaming. We were cheering him on.

We arrived at gate 31 with only seconds to spare. The entire gate area was deserted except for one last flight attendant. She had spotted us in the distance, as our vehicle careened madly toward her gate. I leapt off the electric cart, yelling, "Can I still make this plane? I need to get on this plane!"

The flight attendant scolded me, in mock anger. "Where have you been? You think we can wait all day for you? Get on this plane right now!" She grabbed my ticket, hustled me on board, and slammed the door behind me. I collapsed into my seat, relieved and energized by the whole bizarre experience.

Throughout the entire flight, images of my "dinner" with Luke popped into my head, causing me to laugh out loud. But then I realized the whole thing had happened so quickly that I hadn't really had a chance to thank Luke properly. So as soon as the plane landed I called him at home and said, "Luke, that was such a wonderful thing you did for me. I really want to thank you."

"You don't have to thank me," Luke replied evenly. "Somebody already beat you to it."

"What are you talking about?"

"When I got back to my car, there was a flower on the windshield, with a little note that said, 'Anybody who would do something like that for another person must be a beautiful human being.' "

Luke's offbeat dinner party, which only lasted fifteen minutes, fills me with joy every time I think about it. The spontaneity of the gesture made it especially memorable for me. Of course, I feel good that I have a friend creative enough to dream up and put together a picnic in the parking garage, but even more important, I have a friend willing to go to the trouble of giving me such a gift.

By taking spontaneous action, by giving unexpected gifts of ourselves, we can all create memories for the people we work with. We can let them know they are special to us in ways they will long remember. For whom would you like to create a surprise picnic in the parking garage? You don't need to go to the airport to have a picnic—you can have a picnic right in the office parking lot, or in a park nearby, if your office is in the city. And what if you got another friend or coworker to dress up as a waiter and serve the meal to you and your guest? You can start planning the menu right now . . .

Once a Week: Fifty-Two Ways to Have Fun on the Job

---

19 | GIVE AN EMPLOYEE A SURPRISE DAY OFF

How can managers reward their employees who have worked long hours, night after night, on an important project? John Azzaro, president of Great Speakers lecture bureau, kept his staff of five employees working late one night to complete an important proposal. "I felt badly about the fact that everyone had to stay so late, but we had no alternative," said John. "But I felt even worse that most of my employees would have to go home at that late hour and cook dinner for themselves, or for their families." So as they were leaving the office, John made an announcement: "I really appreciate all the hard work you put in on this project. So get some rest tonight, and don't worry about cooking dinner. I'm calling out for pizza right now, and there will be large pies waiting for all of you when you get home. Extra cheese, anyone?"

At the close of an important project or assignment that has required your salaried employees to work unpaid hours of overtime, think about celebrating the conclusion of the project with pizza, champagne, or ice-cream sundaes. And if the overtime has happened night after night, think about offering your team a paid day off as comp time. If there is an entire work group involved, stagger their days off so you don't get caught shorthanded.

If it is not in your power to award days off, then get creative! On one of your own days off, you can come into work and give one of your hardworking employees an unexpected holiday. Just say to him, "Guess what! You deserve an extra day off, so I'm here to work your shift for you today. Yes, you heard me right. This offer expires in five minutes, so get your butt out of here and go home!"

A group of store managers from Crate and Barrel in Houston, Texas, worked out a modified version of the surprise day off: the "surprise hour off." The managers decided that once a week they would go to one of their sales associates and say, "I want you to have a bonus hour off. I'll cover for you this hour, and I want you to do something for yourself during that time: go to the park, go for a walk, go shopping in the mall. . . . You've been working hard and I appreciate it—and I know you'll come back from this break refreshed and ready to sell some more!"

A word of caution: Don't give up your own day off to create a surprise day off too often, or you can sabotage your own well-being! Even if you love your job, taking time off is an important way of avoiding burnout. Make sure to take your breaks.

Once a Week: Fifty-Two Ways to Have Fun on the Job

 KEEP YOUR HIGH SCHOOL YEARBOOK PHOTO HANDY

Peter C. Mike, materiels management director of the Tucson Medical Center, keeps a color photo of himself mounted on the inside door of a cabinet in his office. No, he's not an egomaniac —the photo was taken moments after Peter had been hit in the face with a pie, and serves a valuable purpose. "Sometimes I will 'accidentally' open the door in the middle of a heavy discussion," he says. "It never fails to get a rise out of the person I'm talking to, and I never tire of laughing about it myself."

Donald Burns, the CEO of an association management company in Sacramento, California, tried something similar. "I'm the president of this company," he said, "but I don't want to have too big an ego about the fact that I'm the boss." So Donald has a framed photograph of himself hung in the conference room, and underneath it is a brass plaque with the words "Our Founder." But it's not a professional portrait—it's the photo from his junior high school yearbook! "I'll tell you something about that picture," he said. "Whenever I'm feeling down about my work, I just take a good look at that dork up on the wall and I think to myself, 'You've come a long way, baby!' Don't stop now!"

Cindy Collins, vice president of the OmniArts company in Nashville, reports that her company has taken this concept one step further. They, too, have a brass plaque with the words "Our Founder" in their office. To go along with it they commissioned one of their artists to paint an original oil painting . . . of a chimpanzee dressed in a suit and tie!

For just a moment now, if you can bear it, think about your own photo in your junior high school or high school yearbook. Think about the "agonies" you were going through back then—the dating, the pimples, the uncontrollable growth spurts, deciding which clothes to wear.

Now think for a moment about the really important problems you are facing in your work life today. Compare your problems today with your high school problems. Can you believe how seriously you took yourself? I guarantee that ten years from now you are going to look back on what you are going through today and say the same thing. We always do the best that we can at any given moment, but at the same time we are continually growing stronger, wiser, and more powerful. Today's urgent problems soon become tomorrow's distant memories.

If you can find a copy of it, tape your own high school graduation photo on the inside of a desk drawer. During times of stress, open the drawer, and take a good look at yourself, face to face. It will give you perspective on the way things change, and a great opportunity to have a good laugh at your own expense. People always say, "Some day I know I'm going to look back at all this and laugh." What you can now say to those people is "Why wait?"

CHAPTER 5

Building a Team: Reward and Recognition

Reward and recognition programs are an essential component of every successful team-building effort. When you are adding an element of fun and play to these programs, it is important to remember the first principle of fun at work: *Think about the specific people involved*. Does this cautionary tale sound familiar to you?

"Our company gives service awards for five and ten years of service," says Delbert Nokia, who works as a manager in the information systems department of a large telecommunications organization. "But nobody really gets excited about the awards. For five years of service, you get to choose a gift from the company gift catalog. Sure, the catalog has expensive gifts, like crystal flower vases, which may be fine for some people. But many of us aren't interested in having cut flowers around the house every day. There are people living in trailers that haven't been completely repaired yet since the last tornado hit us.

They'd much rather have something like a gift certificate to Toys R Us, so they could buy toys for their kids. The only gift that anybody gets really excited about comes at Christmastime, when most people go for the $15 gift certificate to Wal-Mart instead of the company turkey.

"I got a letter opener with a crystal handle for my five-year service award. But I already have a letter opener that I love— it's a little sword that I got in New Orleans. So the classy crystal one sits in my desk drawer. I never even take it out.

"It's like the company knows that they ought to do something to reward us for our years of service so it looks like they care about us. But they don't give it any real thought, and the awards don't help morale at all—in fact, they have the opposite effect. It looks to us like the company is just going through the motions. They could probably even save a lot of money on the crystal gifts if they just took the time to find out what we really want."

The difficulty with a standardized reward and recognition program like Delbert describes is that it is a completely impersonal process. Instead of thinking about the specific people involved, the company provides the same generic awards to everyone. But when an element of fun and play is added to a financial reward or bonus, the experience becomes personalized and much more memorable for the award recipient. Without any additional expenditure the reward can become even more meaningful. When you incorporate an element of fun and play into your corporate awards program, your employees will be delighted not only by the reward itself, but also by the way the reward is presented to them. If you can make the reward and recognition process fun, then your employees will be talking about the event long after it has ended, and you will have multiplied its team-building impact many, many times.

• • •

One month, Dr. Jeff Alexander of the Youthful Tooth dental office calculated that he could give a $200 bonus to each member of his staff. But Dr. Alexander knew that if he just added $200 to each of their paychecks, his staff members would've been excited about it for a little while, then they would've probably used the money for something "practical." So Dr. Alexander invested a bit more time, energy, and creativity, and found a playful way to use the bonus money—a way that had a much more lasting effect.

Dr. Alexander closed down his office for two hours one afternoon and took all thirty-five members of his dental practice to a shopping mall. He gathered the staff around him in a circle and handed them each an envelope containing $200 in cash.

"This is not your money," Dr. Alexander told them. "This is my money. But anything you buy for yourself with this money in the next hour is yours to keep. Here are the rules: You have to spend all the money on gifts for yourself. You have one hour to spend it, and you have to buy at least five different items. Any money you haven't spent in the next hour comes back to me. Go get 'em!"

Dr. Alexander reported that his employees spent the next hour dashing wildly from one store to the next, yelling back and forth to each other about treasures they had found. "If I had just given them the money, they would have put it in the bank or spent it paying bills," says Dr. Alexander. "This was a real treat for them—and it gave me a great feeling, watching them having fun." At the next staff meeting, everyone brought in the presents they had purchased for themselves for a show-and-tell session with the group.

By adding an aura of unexpected excitement to the presentation of the bonus money, Dr. Alexander was able to create a special team-building opportunity for his staff. The trip to the mall gave his employees the chance to interact with one another in a positive social situation completely separate from the normal working environment.

Dr. Alexander's basic concept can be easily adapted to fit a more modest budget. Catherine Jackson, the director of a college food service, was inspired by Dr. Alexander's story to take her own secretary out to lunch at a restaurant in the mall near her office. "During lunch I told her what I appreciated about her —things I hadn't taken the time to tell her before. Then, after lunch was over, I gave her $50 and I said to her, 'Take the next hour off, cruise around the mall, and buy yourself a present from me!' "

And on the opposite end of the financial spectrum, Ford Motor Company spent more than a million dollars in one memorable evening, demonstrating that Dr. Alexander's idea can be easily adapted to fit a more extravagant budget as well. Ford rented out Nordstrom's department store in downtown San Francisco from 6:30 P.M. to midnight one evening and gave $5,000 in spending money to each of its 250 top-selling sales managers, who were in town for a national sales meeting. Ford hired sports celebrities Walter Payton, Tommy Lasorda, and Julius Erving to accompany the sales managers on their shopping spree. According to *San Francisco Chronicle* columnist Herb Caen, "Payton had a ball in the shoe department, acting as salesman to the Fordniks."

Like the staff of the Youthful Tooth, and like Catherine Jackson and her secretary, the Ford sales managers created some shared history together that evening, a history filled with playful memories that they could all reminisce about together in the months that followed.

No matter what your budget, you can make the bonus fun.

Once a Week: Fifty-Two Ways to Have Fun on the Job

---

21   PUT YOURSELF IN GOOD COMPANY

By definition, a bank is hardly anybody's idea of a happy-go-lucky institution. But the Wells Fargo Bank in northern California found an excellent way to incorporate a sense of fun and reward into recognizing its employees. The Wells Fargo program, called "In Good Company," was designed to encourage all Wells Fargo employees to honor their coworkers. "In Good Company" was a reward and recognition program in which all the award recipients were picked by their peers.

In Phase One, entitled appropriately enough "A Cash Award," all the full-time employees of the bank received a $500 bonus; the hourly employees each received a $50 bonus. But it was in Phase Two, called "A Way to Thank Others," that the bank created a truly original event. All bank employees were given a $35 certificate to award to the coworker of their choice. "Working with good colleagues helps make all our days more fulfilling, and being in their company helps us achieve more," wrote the bank in announcing the program. "Phase Two of 'We're in Good Company' provides an opportunity to say a special *Thanks with Cash* to a colleague who has helped boost your efforts on the job.

"Here's How: If you're salaried, in a few days you'll receive a blank certificate with a tear-off coupon attached. The certificate states, 'You're Good Company,' and it is yours to present to someone you'd like to single out for thanks. On the certificate and coupon, fill in that person's name and indicate just what quality or qualities you appreciate in your coworker. Has that person been an inspiration to you? Always cooperative? Always there with just the right bit of information you need? Someone who makes the office run smoothly, or someone who always lightens the atmosphere? It's your opportunity to reflect on and acknowledge just what and who really makes things tick.

"Present the certificate to your chosen recipient. And bear in mind that you are giving more than just a piece of paper: The coupon is redeemable for $35. And there's no limit to the number of coupons an employee may receive and redeem."

The "You're Good Company" coupon was very simple to award. Wells Fargo helped its employees decide who deserved to be given the $35 bonus by designing a coupon that contained a checklist of categories for which it could be awarded. The coupon read:

This coupon is my way of saying thank you for . . .

___ Putting the customer first

___ Always putting in the extra effort

___ Working so creatively

___ Taking the initiative

___ Coming through every time

___ Other:

___ Helping me get the job done

___ Being someone I can rely on

___ Making it fun

___ Inspiring me to excel

___ Daring to do it right

The bank supported the program with an "In Good Company" newsletter and a telephone hotline for questions about procedures or eligibility. Then, after all the certificates had been awarded and tabulated, Wells Fargo gave the thirty-one employees who had received the most coupons some extra special attention. All thirty-one were profiled in issues of the "In Good Company" newsletter, accompanied by photographs and glowing testimonials from their coworkers. Then they were honored at an awards banquet hosted by the chairman of the board, Carl Reichardt, and the president of the bank, Paul Hazen.

At the banquet, the award recipients were given their choice of 101 different awards. The awards list was widely circulated throughout the bank and included an imaginative array of choices that fell into a wide range of categories, including:

Unusual Time with Senior Executives ("A $200 shopping spree at Carl Reichardt's favorite store, Banana Republic, and lunch at Paul Hazen's favorite lunch spot, Burger King—hosted by Carl and Paul"; "Carl Reichardt, Paul Hazen, or one of the vice chairmen does *your* job for a day—you train and supervise")

Family Assistance ("$1000 worth of elder care"; "twenty hours of tutoring for your child")

Hedonism ("A two-hour body massage on April 15"; "two pounds of Mrs. Field's cookies each month for the next year")

Field Trips ("A weekend for two in the wine country and a case of wine"; "a makeover and pampering at the local salon of your choice")

Office Fun ("A balloon bouquet delivered to your office every month for a year"; "morning coffee and croissants for your entire department served by your group head")

Family Fun ("A birthday party for a child on the Wells Fargo Stagecoach"; "four annual passes to Disneyland, Magic Mountain, Knott's Berry Farm, Sea World, Great America, or Marine World Africa USA")

Physical Fitness ("New workout clothes, and a morning at the gym"; "the initial membership fee and first month's dues for a spa or health club")

Cultural Improvement ("A world globe on a stand"; "one year's worth of selections from a book club")

Entertainment ("Two tickets for a New Year's Eve gala in your city"; "local limousine service to a Dodger game, Dodger jackets, box seats, hot dogs, and beer or soda for you and your son or daughter")

Unexpected Gifts ("A bag of fertilizer for your garden personally supplied by the horses that pull the Wells Fargo stagecoach"; "a year's worth of pantyhose")

And my personal favorite, because it gives you a kind of ***Corporate Immortality:*** "A menu item named in your honor by the Wells Fargo cafeteria."

(For the complete list of 101 awards, see page 123.)

22 | ESTABLISH PEER REWARD AND RECOGNITION

How would a program like Wells Fargo's "In Good Company" work with a smaller business, or with an individual department of a larger corporation that may not have the budget to replicate the entire scope of the program? The core idea of peer reward and recognition is one that can be creatively adjusted to fit many varied budgets. Two organizations that have found ways to adapt this basic concept to fit their own needs are Pacific Bell Directory, in northern California, and Miramar Publications, a magazine publisher in San Diego.

Pacific Bell Directory created the "Gotcha!" award, an award that could be presented by anyone in the company to a colleague "caught" doing exceptional work. Each employee was given a supply of "Gotcha!" certificates worth $5 apiece. Management and nonmanagement employees alike were given the same number of certificates to award, and as soon as someone caught a coworker doing a great job, he or she was instructed to yell "Gotcha!" and to immediately sign the $5 certificate over to that person as an instantaneous reward.

"The $5 is just a token," says Pacific Bell Directory employee Vance Lampert. "Everybody knows that. The important thing is that it feels great to know that your hard work is being noticed by the people you're working with. I had completely forgotten about the whole 'Gotcha!' thing the first time one was given to me, but the person who awarded it to me made a big deal about it, and announced it in front of everybody. You know, 'Stop the presses, we've got a "Gotcha!" thing happening here.' I kept smiling about it all day."

Miramar Publications, which has seventy-five employees, used a variation of the "In Good Company" program as a part of its year-end reward and recognition program. The company gave $10 to each of its nonmanagement employees and $100 to each of its managers. The instructions were for each employee to write an anonymous note of thanks or a note of praise to a fellow employee and to enclose the cash along with it. According to Miramar president Tim Novoselski, some of the participants had a hard time deciding among their favorite candidates. "One of the managers came to me and said, 'I just can't decide between two of the women I supervise—they've both done so well this year. They both deserve the money. How about if I write two letters and I just give $50 to each of them?' "

"I told him that he couldn't do that," said Tim. "I reminded him that the idea of the program was to give somebody $100. You feel really good when you get $100 out of the blue. So I told him that he'd just have to choose between the two of them."

"I just can't do that," he said.

"Then I guess you're just going to have to take another hundred bucks out of your own pocket!" Tim told him. "I was half-joking—I never really thought he'd do it. But his eyes lit up as soon as I suggested it. 'You're absolutely right,' he said. 'That's exactly what I'm going to to do.' And that's what he did."

I would bet that the $100 that came from the manager's own pocket made even more of an impression on both the giver and the receiver of the reward than the $100 that came from the company. In making a gesture of appreciation to a fellow employee, the spirit in which the gift is given is often more important than the gift itself.

Even a silly little gesture where the monetary value of the gift is insignificant can still have a big effect on the recipient, if it's done in a spirit of sincerity and caring. In many cases, the intention with which a gift is given speaks much more loudly than the actual gift itself. There is a big difference between a generic, insincere, silly little gesture and a genuine, heartfelt, silly little gesture!

Once a Week: Fifty-Two Ways to Have Fun on the Job

23 | PACK WITH PRIDE

Reward and recognition do not always have to involve additional expenditures of money. It is not always practical, nor is it even appropriate, to give a financial reward for minor, everyday accomplishments that are an expected part of one's job description. But it is always appropriate to give recognition for a job well done.

If we define recognition as "shining a spotlight of positive attention on a coworker," then recognition can be something as simple as sending a note of appreciation to a member of your team for a job well done. Recognition can even be communicated by tone of voice or word selection. One manager told me that, "I was at a cocktail party with my boss, and he introduced me to one of his colleagues as 'someone who works *with* me,' instead of 'someone who works *for* me.' That made all the difference in the world."

Sometimes recognition needs to be communicated in private: some of your employees or coworkers will be embarrassed by too much public attention, and it is always important to be sensitive to that possibility. And, if the recognition is coupled with an attitude of fun, originality, and celebration, it will, of course, have an even greater impact.

At the Crate and Barrel warehouse in Newark, New Jersey, East Coast distribution manager Al Cheli felt that his warehouse team deserved a higher profile within the company. After all, they were the ones constantly laboring behind the scenes, packing the trucks with furniture and housewares and sending the inventory out to the stores every day. But they never got any feedback or any appreciation from *their* customers—the store managers. So Al created the "Packed with Pride" campaign. He had a huge banner made to read "Packed with Pride," which was hung on the loading dock. After each truck was packed, Al would snap a Polaroid of the loading team standing under the sign. They included this photo along with the shipment.

At the management meeting where Al announced his idea, the store managers spontaneously rose and gave him an enthusiastic standing ovation. Now, he says, his team gets personalized notes of support and thanks from the store managers. "They know who we are now. We're no longer just an anonymous warehouse crew," he says. "And we get a big kick out of hearing from the stores. The best response we got was when one store sent us their own group portrait—they called it 'Un-Packed with Pride!' "

24 BECOME A FREQUENT FLYER

Bob Rich and Monte Anglin, two managers in IBM's Storage Systems division in San Jose, California, wanted to focus their organization on daily rewards and recognition. "We wanted to increase the number of thank-you's that people expressed to each other every day," remembers Monte. In order to encourage this, Bob invented the IBM Frequent Flyer program, which he modeled on the frequent flyer programs of the airlines.

First, Bob bought a trophy featuring a model airplane for every department in the organization. To get things started, he asked one manager in each department to award the trophy to one of the people who reported to him or her. There were only two simple rules to follow: (1) You have to give up your flight on Friday, and (2) you have to file a flight plan.

These two rules meant that (1) on every Friday the recipients of the trophy had to award it to someone else in the organization, and (2) at the time of awarding the trophy, you had to write a brief description ("a flight plan") of what the new recipient had done to deserve the award. The flight plan was then filed in the central frequent flyer administration office, where the recipient of the trophy would be credited with 1,000 frequent flyer miles, and the person awarding the trophy would be credited with 500 frequent flyer miles.

Just as in the airline frequent flyer programs, these miles could then be exchanged for free gifts. Starting at the 2,500-mile award level, the participants could choose from a catalog of gifts embossed with the IBM logo, from coffee cups and folding umbrellas to a set of Cross pens or a matching set of luggage. At the 20,000-mile level, the participants were able to cash in their mileage awards for a day off with pay. As might be expected, the longtime employees, who had accumulated more vacation time than they would probably use anyway, were more likely to choose the catalog gifts, while the new hires were eager to win the days off.

After the initial round, when the trophies were awarded by the managers, the program became a true peer reward and recognition effort, with both management and staff participating equally. In order to encourage people to look outside of their immediate circle of coworkers, double mileage was awarded for presenting the trophy to someone outside of your own department. A list of "high flyers" was posted every week on the company bulletin board, featuring those employees who had accumulated high mileage totals. To foster cooperation between the various working units, second-line managers were empowered to award bonus miles to employees on teams other than their own, in appreciation for the support and assistance they provided on projects.

At first, the participants spent most of their time awarding the trophies for all the things that had happened in the past year that had gone uncelebrated. Eventually, however, the participants ran out of "easy" reasons to present the trophy and had to begin observing each other more closely.

A year after the program's inception, not only had the IBM Storage Systems employees found ample reason to award the trophy to each other, they had also begun praising one another verbally much more often than they had before. Even when they didn't have the trophy in their possession to give as an award, Monte observed, the employees continued to openly and spontaneously acknowledge one another. The Frequent Flyer program had provided a practical launching pad so "reward and recognition on a daily basis" could become an everyday reality.

<hr>

Once a Week: Fifty-Two Ways to Have Fun on the Job

<hr>

25 | SCRATCH AND WIN

Soon after the CVS drugstore chain had completed an extensive renovation of all its stores in the Washington, D.C., area, CVS management wanted to ensure that the customers attracted by the "new and improved stores" would find an even higher quality of customer service. So Larry Merlo, the senior vice president for stores, initiated a "scratch and win" promotion to help the CVS store managers reinforce good customer service.

The concept was simple and fun. CVS managers and district supervisors were given books of "scratch and win" tickets that they were to hand out as on-the-spot rewards to employees performing outstanding acts of customer service. In addition, the store managers were asked to be specific in their verbal appreciation of the employees' good service; when they handed out the tickets, they were to say things like, "You responded very quickly to the call to open your checkout register. Good job!"

"We found that it wasn't necessary to put a large dollar amount on the value of the tickets," said Fred McGrail, the director of communications for CVS. "It wasn't how much the tickets were worth, it was the fun way they were presented that made them meaningful. Most of the prizes actually cost us less than a dollar each." When an employee received the ticket, she would scratch off the CVS logo, and underneath would be one of a number of prizes, for example, (1) choosing your own duties on an upcoming shift, (2) a free soda, (3) a free snack food (like a bag of chips), or (4) 50 cents off the purchase of any item in the store.

Larry Merlo reported that one immediate, important effect of the promotion was that store managers who had previously had trouble praising employees found it simple to use this structured way of saying "thank you." Because of the ticket system, the amount of positive feedback that the store employees received increased immediately.

And store employees who received more than one ticket would often share with their fellow workers the reasons they had been rewarded: "This is my third one. I got one for straightening up the vitamins in the pharmacy, and another one for helping a customer find the right brand of aspirin for her kid." Employees trading stories about the tickets "helped reinforce our standards of good customer service on the peer-to-peer level," added Larry Merlo.

But as with any innovative idea, "You don't want to overuse it or it loses its impact," said Merlo. "So after three months, we pulled the scratch tickets from the stores. Then, six months later, at Christmas, which is our peak season, we brought them back again. But this time we included all the stores in our system, not just the ones in Washington, D.C." Merlo then posed an interesting question: How do you keep up the level of positive reinforcement from the store managers when they are not participating in company-wide promotions like the scratch and win tickets? What should they do in the six months in between?

"We encouraged our store managers to take some discretionary funds and be inventive in the ways they rewarded their employees. Some store managers bought twenty tickets to the local cinema and handed them out as on-the-spot rewards to their employees. Or they awarded free housecleaning certificates in appreciation for a special job well done. They took the basic idea of the scratch and win tickets, and the idea of instantaneous reward, and they invented their own version of it. They know we'll always make monies available for things like that."

Once a Week: Fifty-Two Ways to Have Fun on the Job

---

26 | THANK THE SUPPORT PEOPLE

Over the course of a three-month period, Marilyn Waters, president of Watermark Public Relations in Melbourne, Florida, had to ask her staff to work long hours on several important projects. When the projects had been successfully completed, Marilyn wanted to express her appreciation to her staff for working beyond the call of duty. But not only did she want to thank them, she also wanted to express her appreciation to the "support people at home"—the spouses and parents of her employees.

Marilyn wrote six personalized letters (five to the spouses of five of her employees and one to the parents of a young man who still lived at home). The letters explained specifically how much it meant to Marilyn to have someone like their spouse (or son) on her staff, and she thanked them for putting up with the long hours at the office.

Here is a sample of one of Marilyn's letters, to the husband of an account executive:

> Dear Claude,
>
> I wanted to write and let you know how much positive energy Monica adds to Watermark. She is always working to give our clients the best service and to enhance the reputation of our company—things she does very well.
>
> It's a real pleasure to watch Monica grow and develop her expertise. She's constantly looking for ways to improve herself and our entire staff—and her attitude is contagious.
>
> I also want to thank you for your support! Sometimes our hours are crazy (as well as our staff) and I thank you for being understanding of Monica and Watermark during these times.
>
> I try hard to let all my employees know how much I value them—and by sharing these thoughts with you, it gives me yet another way to thank Monica.
>
> Warmly,
> Marilyn Waters

Marilyn reported that she received several notes and phone calls after her letters had been received. The delighted spouses wanted to let her know how much it meant to them that their loved ones were so appreciated at work.

27 | CULTIVATE THE HUMAN TOUCH

Jesse M. Smith, executive director of the American Compensation Association in Scottsdale, Arizona, developed an Outstanding Achievement Award, which is simple in concept but broad in effect, for the members of his staff. Every member of the staff is eligible to be nominated for this award (which carries a cash prize ranging from several hundred to several thousand dollars) by any of his or her coworkers. Each nomination is then reviewed by the awards committee, which consists of representatives from each of the six staff teams; the award is then presented at a special ceremony.

Jesse remembers the first award ceremony very well. "I called a meeting of the entire staff of fifty-five people, and I stood with the recipient at the front of the room. I put my arm around her shoulder as I read the committee's statement detailing the good work she had done. Then I presented her with the monetary award and said a few words myself about how delighted I was to have her on staff.

"After it was all over, I asked her what the ceremony had been like for her. And you know what she told me? She said what meant the most to her was not the prize money and not all the attention she received but the fact that I had my arm around her the whole time."

Of course, the question of whether or not it is appropriate to have any sort of physical contact between two coworkers must always be approached with respect and sensitivity. But when done sincerely and appropriately, sometimes the human touch can communicate appreciation more strongly than anything else.

Once a Week: Fifty-Two Ways to Have Fun on the Job

---

28 | PLAY CHILDHOOD GAMES

Oftentimes, the best thing to do when you're under pressure is to take a break, get away from the job at hand, and recharge your batteries. Force yourself to leave things alone for a while: a few minutes of respite from a difficult task can save hours of brain-numbed wrestling with a problem situation. The fact is, sometimes the best way to move ahead is to stop altogether for a while.

One simple strategy for organizing a break is to play your favorite childhood games, especially at a crucial time during a taxing project. Peter Frid, assistant general manager of KTOO-TV in Juneau, Alaska, was part of an endless fund-raising meeting chaired by Don Rinker, president and general manager of the station. After hours of difficult financial negotiation, Don looked around the room and saw glazed, bloodshot eyes staring back at him. He firmly announced, "We need a break!"

Don dragged Peter out into the hallway and challenged him to a game of pitching pennies. When the two of them got down on their hands and knees they stopped thinking about raising hundreds of thousands of dollars for the station. Their concern was more immediate—who would win the next penny?

Peg Bargon, who is also in the educational television industry, found a way to use a familiar children's game for relief from the tension of working under a deadline. One day Peg was under tremendous pressure at work, and she sensed that the rest of the staff was at the threshold of a stress explosion too. So Peg, who is a marketing representative at the Educational Program Service in Columbia, South Carolina, went to the closest drugstore, bought a bag of marbles, and brought them into work. Then she challenged the rest of the staff to a contest.

"The best thing was that nobody really remembered how to play," said Peg, "so we just got down on the floor and made up our own crazy games. It was more about laughing and being together than winning or losing, and it was just what we needed. Every so often we've tried it again."

Howard Roth, the editor-in-chief of *Manufacturing Week,* gathered his staff together at 3 P.M., one hour before the deadline for putting the paper to bed. Roth put on some loud music and challenged them all to a breakdancing contest. "We'd been in high gear for two days straight," recalls Roth. "Most of us had been in the office until eight or ten the night before, and we were fried.

"Of course, no one could remember exactly what breakdancing actually looked like, since it hasn't been around for quite a few years. Not that any of us could do it very well anyway, even in our prime. But we were all so punchy that we just laughed and laughed at one another's feeble efforts to gyrate around on the office floor. At one point we were laughing so hard we couldn't even stand up. By the time it was over we were all on the floor, with tears in our eyes.

"It was a great energizer. And, of course, we got the paper out on time."

Reward yourself for working hard. Remember to take a break, play some games, have some fun. Then go back, refreshed, to the job at hand.

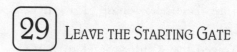

Once a Week: Fifty-Two Ways to Have Fun on the Job

29 | LEAVE THE STARTING GATE

Whenever a salesperson closes a deal or gets a qualified lead in the IBM Southern Trading Area office (which covers Alabama, Mississippi, and Georgia), she races over to a large gong and smashes it with a mallet so that everyone in the office knows about her sale right away. Then the salesperson heads over to the "Tele-Sales Arena," an elaborate miniature racetrack. There she finds a line of toy horses poised at the starting gate. She looks carefully at the photographs of the "jockeys" mounted on the saddles until she recognizes a photograph of her own head seated on one of the horses. She moves that horse out of the starting gate and onto the track. If she makes another sale later in the day, she bangs the gong again, and places a tiny picture of the state in which the second sale occurred under her toy horse.

"The idea is to get each of our salespeople 'out of the gate' every day," says Karen Donnelly, who is an executive in the Client Satisfaction Center. "Some days we'll set it up so that the first person out of the gate gets a free lunch. Other days the first state team out of the gate gets a free lunch together. We save the biggest celebrations for the days when everybody in the office gets out of the gate."

Each morning the sales leader from the previous day has his or her photo taken with the vice president of sales. Then he or she chooses one of the other salespeople to play the tuba to accompany the morning's sales song. "Of course, none of us can actually play the tuba," admits Karen Donnelly, "so mostly it's just a matter of puffing along with the wrong notes in the right rhythm."

"And what exactly are these sales songs?" I asked her, intrigued.

"Oh, we've just changed the words around to nursery rhymes and fifties rock-and-roll songs, and we start off each morning by singing one together."

". . . And what might be an example of one of these songs?" I asked.

"You really want to know? Well, this morning, for example, we started out with our own special version of 'Row Row Row Your Boat.' Now, you have to imagine the tuba accompaniment to go along with this song:

> *Close close close your leads*
> *And we'll all succeed . . .*
> *Merrily, merrily, merrily, merrily*
> *Working like a team!"*

As soon as Karen stopped singing, we both started laughing. "And then what happens?" I asked her.

"And then what happens? As soon as the song is over, we all hit the phones and try to be the first one to ring the gong and get out of the gate!"

The Wells Fargo "In Good Company" Program:
The Complete List of Awards

1. An American Gold Eagle coin
2. A day at work with a senior executive
3. Five shares of Wells Fargo stock
4. A star named after you
5. $200 contribution to your retirement account
6. A day on a Wells Fargo TV commercial shoot
7. A party for ten in your honor staged by Wells Fargo Communicating Arts
8. A bag of fertilizer for your garden personally supplied by the horses that pull the Wells Fargo stagecoach
9. A barrel of peanuts
10. A $500 Series EE savings bond
11. The "shotgun" position on the stagecoach in a local parade
12. A dinner for two at a restaurant of your choice
13. A birthday party for a child on the Wells Fargo stagecoach
14. A visit from Reichardt or Hazen to your branch or department to attend your staff meeting and answer all questions
15. An all-expense-paid trip for one to a Wells Fargo shareholders meeting with an introduction to the shareholders
16. A monogrammed brass stamp box with 200 stamps
17. A photographic portrait of you or your family on the Wells Fargo stagecoach
18. A week off with pay
19. A dozen bleacher seats at a regularly scheduled night or weekend sports event
20. A speech with question-and-answer session by a senior executive for your civic or service organization
21. A visit to your child's school or club meeting by a senior executive
22. Software for your home computer

23. A $500 donation made in your name to the nonprofit organization of your choice
24. Two tickets for a New Year's Eve gala in your city
25. A videotape library of award-winning Wells Fargo TV commercials
26. A "mini-scholarship" for a local class or seminar of your choice offered outside Wells Fargo and, if held during scheduled work hours, time off with pay to attend
27. A world globe on a stand
28. A $200 shopping spree at Carl Reichardt's favorite store, Banana Republic, and lunch at Paul Hazen's favorite lunch spot, Burger King—hosted by Carl and Paul
29. Four seats for the 1990 Rose Parade in the Wells Fargo grandstand at Colorado and Orange Grove, and invitations to a VIP party
30. A cotton candy maker
31. Once-a-month housecleaning service for six months
32. A career counseling interview with a senior manager of your choice
33. A camera and photograph album
34. A color monitor for your home computer
35. A new golf outfit and golf and lunch with Jack Grundhofer
36. Payment of your December home mortgage, lease, or rent
37. Cat or dog food supply for a year
38. A month's worth of tickets for your commute on BART/MUNI/RTD or your local public transportation system
39. Tea at I. Magnin with Ellen Newman, board member, and a $200 I. Magnin gift certificate
40. A California history lesson and guided tour of Wells Fargo's Los Angeles or San Francisco History Museum, souvenirs, and lunch for your child's class or club
41. A photographic portrait of you with Carl Reichardt and Paul Hazen
42. Free income tax preparation

43. A two-hour body massage on April 15
44. Use of Wells Fargo Communicating Arts to design your personal stationery, holiday card, or a logo or poster for your club or civic organization and $200 in printing costs
45. The initial membership fee and first month's dues for a spa or health club
46. First-year fee for personalized license plates
47. Two round-trip coach airline tickets to anywhere in your state of residence
48. An autographed copy of the *Wells Fargo Employee Handbook* from the staff who wrote it
49. Two season tickets for the sports team of your choice (if available)
50. A mountain bike
51. $1,000 worth of elder care
52. A $200 shopping spree at a store of your choice
53. A coffee maker, grinder, and beans
54. Twenty hours of music or sports lessons for you or your child
55. Four annual passes to Disneyland, Magic Mountain, Knott's Berry Farm, Sea World, Great America, or Marine World Africa USA
56. Two pounds of Mrs. Field's cookies each month for the next year
57. An exercycle and sweat outfit
58. Three three-day weekends with the third day paid
59. Two weeks of child care
60. $200 credit on your Wells Fargo VISA or MasterCard
61. Carl Reichardt, Paul Hazen, or one of the vice chairmen does *your* job for a day—you train and supervise
62. Two season tickets for an available cultural series of your choice
63. Twenty hours of tutoring for your child
64. A lifetime supply of "We're in Good Company!" pens
65. A tour of Geyser Peak Winery with Henry Trione, board member, former chairman of the board of the former Wells Fargo

Mortgage Company, and current chairman of the executive committee of Geyser Peak

66. Flowers delivered to you once a month during the year
67. Two sessions with a financial planner of your choice
68. A one-year subscription to *Money* magazine
69. Two nights in a hotel or resort of your choice
70. One year's worth of selections from a record and tape club
71. Four movie tickets a month for a year
72. New tennis garb and tennis and lunch with Bob Joss
73. One month paid parking
74. A leather set of *World Book Encyclopedia*
75. Five pounds of jelly beans—18 different flavors
76. New workout clothes, a morning at the gym, and lunch with Bill Zuendt
77. $200 in groceries
78. A makeover and pampering at the local salon of your choice
79. Local limousine service to a Dodger game, Dodger jackets, box seats, hot dogs, and beer or soda for you and your son or daughter
80. One year's worth of selections from a book club
81. A monogrammed briefcase or overnight bag
82. Morning coffee and croissants for your entire department served by your group head
83. Plants of your choice for your home or office
84. A weekend for two in the wine country and a case of wine
85. A membership in the Snack of the Month Club
86. One month's paid telephone bills
87. Cooking lessons from a local cooking school
88. A menu item named in your honor by the Wells Fargo cafeteria
89. A monogrammed desk set
90. Your Wells Fargo–sponsored health-care premiums paid for one year
91. A phone answering machine
92. Two pairs of shoes: one for work and one for play

93. A hot air balloon ride for two
94. Grooming for your pet for a year
95. A week's worth of temporary help for the nonprofit organization of your choice
96. Learn how a stagecoach is built from the man who builds Wells Fargo's
97. A year's worth of pantyhose
98. One complete automobile detailing
99. A set of 1988 Wells Fargo phonebooks and a paper shredder
100. A balloon bouquet delivered to your office every month for a year
101. A pedigree Dalmatian puppy

CHAPTER 6

Think Big:
Company-Wide Initiatives

We have already seen in the stories of Chris Wells and Kirt Womack that it is possible to bring fun to work even in the face of unsupportive management. But imagine how much easier it would be if the upper management of a company were completely supportive—in fact, encouraging—of fun at work. I had the good fortune to hear Gordon Segal, president of the national housewares retail chain Crate and Barrel, address his management team on this very subject.

"This company is like a family," he told them. "Most of the people in this room have been with this company ten years and longer. And if you're going to continue to grow in your jobs, then your work has to continue to be fun for you. We have very high standards for this company and very demanding goals for our sales associates. And if they are going to put forth the extra effort to meet our high standards, then you're going to have to make sure that their jobs are fun for them!

"I want this to be an entrepreneurial company. I've always believed that it's better to ask for forgiveness than to ask for permission. To make fun happen, you're going to have to take some risks, which means that you're going to fail now and again. That's okay, it's expected. From now on, I give you my permission to throw your inhibitions to the wind and to make your stores a fun place to work. And this is the last time I want to have to grant you permission! . . . Unless, of course, what you want to do costs more than a couple of thousand dollars. . . . Then you'd better run it by Suzie Muellman, our human resources director, first!"

The managers were given a chance that day to brainstorm answers to the question, "What can you do in the next two weeks to bring fun, joy, celebration, reward, and recognition to the people you work with?" With the open support and encouragement from upper management, the Crate and Barrel managers unleashed their creative thinking. Each manager pledged to implement at least one of his or her brainstormed ideas within the next two weeks following the meeting. Here is a sampling of what they came up with:

- "I'm going to pick up a lottery ticket on the way to work and attach it to the handle of the broom in the back of the store. That way, the lucky first person who picks up the broom to sweep up the store will win an unexpected prize."
- "There's a tree in our parking lot that drips some kind of sticky resin on the cars parked underneath it. During lunch hour, I'm going to wash the windshields of those cars."

- "I'm going to call a surprise fifteen-minute basketball break during the most stressful truck unloading time at the furniture warehouse."
- "I'm going to cook an omelet breakfast for my staff one morning, and for lunch one day I'll set up a staff barbecue outside the back door of the store."
- "I'm going to install a customer service board, and post customer comment cards and letters about outstanding customer service they received from employees in the store."

Of course, the company that practically owns the franchise on organized fun at work is Ben and Jerry's Ice Cream in Waterbury, Vermont. Company founders Ben Cohen and Jerry Greenfield set the tone of corporate irreverence early in the company's existence. At one of the first annual stockholders' meetings, Ben, dressed in a turban and introduced as the famous mystic Habeeni Ben Coheeni, lay down between two chairs with a concrete block balanced on his stomach. Jerry, who had taken a class in carnival tricks in college, walked on stage armed with a sledgehammer and proceeded to smash the concrete block into numerous pieces, to the general acclaim of the stockholders.

Ben and Jerry's has a permanent committee, called the Joy Gang, that plans fun activities for its employees. The Joy Gang is headed by a full-time coordinator, Sean Greenwood, whose title is "Grand Poobah." (The title of Grand Poobah originally belonged to Jerry Greenfield, who handed it down to Peter Lind, the company's head of R&D, who then passed it on to Sean, who doubles as director of corporate communications.)

At any one time the Joy Gang will consist of Sean, who acts as point person for the group, and ten to twenty volunteers from throughout the 600-person organization. The Joy Gang has three primary functions. The first is to review applications for "joy grants" of up to $500 for individuals or departments who want to bring more joy to their workplace. Past recipients have used the money to buy a stereo system for the crew in the production room, and to buy a hot cocoa machine for the freezer crew, who have to work in below-freezing temperatures.

"People always enjoy surprises," says Sean, and so the second function of the Joy Gang is to "create permanent spontaneity." Sean and his team of "joy ninjas" come to work at odd hours and leave surprises—like candy hearts and flowers on Valentine's Day—for coworkers to find.

The third function is the most elaborate: creating pre-planned contests and events that are announced in advance to the Ben and Jerry's community. On Elvis Presley's birthday, for example, the Joy Gang hired an Elvis impersonator, served an Elvis cake, and held Elvis look-alike, sound-alike, and sneer-alike contests (the winners received statuettes of Elvis). Former company president Fred Lager came to work dressed as Elvis that day and handed out snacks to unsuspecting tourists getting the tour of the factory.

Since casual dress is the norm at Ben and Jerry's, the Joy Gang sponsored "Clash Dressing Day," where employees were encouraged to put together their worst matching outfits. And for something completely different, the Joy Gang sponsored "Corporate Day," where employees were encouraged to come to work in suits, ties, dresses, and heels. "Ironically, that one was a big hit," muses Sean. "People are always asking me when we're going to have 'dress-up day' again!"

During his ten years at Ben and Jerry's, Sean has seen the company grow from fifty employees to six hundred. "As we

grow larger, the Joy Gang helps keep up the spirit and the
energy of the organization. Our events help reinforce the company culture of being yourself, being creative, and feeling comfortable with whatever your role is in the company. I feel like
we're helping to knock down the barriers between people, to
help them connect, and to maintain a spirit of creativity."

Another CEO who openly embraces the concept of fun at work
is Jim Malone. When I first met him, Jim was the CEO of
Puralator Filter; he later became the CEO of Grimes Aerospace
in Columbus, Ohio. Jim Malone's corporate motto in both
companies was widely disseminated to the employees throughout all levels of the organization. His motto was "Profit,
Growth, and Fun."

Profit, growth, and fun—three concepts that are seldom
linked together in business, but make so much *sense*. It's a
rather simple concept; an organization where the employees are
having fun is going to be highly productive and (if managed
properly) profitable. And "growth" in this sense is double-
sided: it refers not only to the financial growth of the company
but to the personal growth of its employees, as well.

A manager is generally concerned with two very different
things: management and leadership. Management involves the
financial growth of the company; leadership entails the personal
growth of employees. As a leader, you have the incredible opportunity to help shape the lives of the people you supervise.
Part of the unspoken contract between a company and its employees is that the employees will come away from their jobs
with not only financial enrichment but also personal enrichment. They will leave the company more intellectually devel-

oped, more technically skilled, and more personally powerful—as individuals—than when they began.

This chapter contains a number of activities in which your entire organization (or division) can participate together. By nature, these activities need the sanction and participation of the management team in your organization. By incorporating activities like these into your everyday work life, you can develop a sense of fun at work that can help you achieve both of your management goals: increased productivity and financial growth as a manager; increased teamwork and personal growth as a leader.

Once a Week: Fifty-Two Ways to Have Fun on the Job

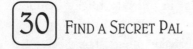

30 | FIND A SECRET PAL

Sometimes it is helpful to organize a structured activity that legitimizes the concept of having fun together. If everyone in the organization participates in this activity together, then no one has to take the risk of being a "pioneer." One such simple and effective activity is the "Secret Pal."

Have everyone in your organization jot down on a sheet of paper his or her name, phone number, birthday, and a short list of things he or she likes (such as roses, chocolate, the Giants, the ballet, postcards, movies, colorful vests, etc.). Fold the sheets of paper and put them all in a hat. Have each person pick a sheet out of the hat, making sure that no one has picked herself. (If so, all slips go back in the hat and you must start again.)

Once all the sheets have been distributed and you have selected someone else's name, you are that person's Secret Pal. Over the course of the Secret Pal experience (somewhere between two weeks and three months is a good length of time) your mission is to do creative, spontaneous, fun, and enlivening things for your partner . . . all anonymously, of course. Part of the fun is that at the same time you are being a secret pal to someone, someone else is being a secret pal to you.

One of the real challenges of this exercise is to keep your identity a secret. In an effort to throw a partner off, Secret Pal participants have sneaked out of meetings early to leave things on their partner's desk, and have come in early or stayed late at work to avoid being caught in the act. Many Secret Pals I've known have gone to great lengths to enlist friends from all over the world to write postcards in untraceable handwriting and to mail packages from odd locations in order to totally befuddle their partners.

When we tried it in the Playfair office, The Secret Pal unleashed a whirlwind of creative energy. One woman came to work early in the morning, turned on her computer, and discovered an unusual message that read: "GO TO YOUR MAIL-BOX!" In her mailbox she found homemade cookies that her secret pal had baked the night before.

Another woman received a Valentine from her secret pal —in September! "I just couldn't wait until February to let you know how lovable you are!" said the card.

One man returned home after work and was greeted by his overjoyed spouse, who threw her arms around him and said, "Oh, honey, thanks for the roses! They're just so beautiful!"

"Roses?" he thought to himself, "I don't know anything about any roses." But then he realized that his Secret Pal had sent roses home to his wife in his name. (Or at least he hoped so!)

Another man in the company who was famous for cooking homemade ribs at our Playfair picnics was stunned to find a package of ribs delivered to his desk in the middle of the day . . . via Federal Express!

My own Secret Pal must have seen me wearing my favorite "Did a Comet Kill the Dinosaurs?" sweatshirt, because he immediately embraced the dinosaur motif. I came into work one day and found a giant inflatable stegosaurus waiting for me on my desk. This was followed by dino-snap cookies planted in my desk drawers and little rubber dinosaurs in my jacket pockets. He even went so far as to mail a pair of brontosaurus boxer shorts to my home. (I had assumed that my Secret Pal was part of our Berkeley, California, office, since many dinosaur artifacts kept appearing in and around my desk. As I looked at the dinosaur items for clues to their sender's identity, however, I noticed that while the boxers had been mailed from California, they had a "Made in Canada" label on them. That was my first big clue that my Secret Pal was in fact based in our Vancouver office, and that he or she was working hand in glove with an accomplice in the California office where I worked.)

At our staff re-treat several months after we had begun the Secret Pal process, the Playfair organization held its "Secret Pal Revealed" meeting. With all the participants seated in a circle, each person was asked to point to the one person suspected of being his or her Secret Pal. Then, one by one, each of the Secret Pals performed some action in front of the group that only his or her own partner would recognize as a clue to his or her identity. Karen Kolberg, for example, had cut up a photograph of her partner, Jeffrey Randall, and made it into a jigsaw puzzle. She had then sent the various pieces of the puzzle to Jeffrey from carefully disguised postmark locations all around the country. The final piece that he needed to complete the jigsaw puzzle was a photo of his nose. At the moment of truth, Karen taped the jigsaw photo of his nose on top of her own nose, and walked slowly around the circle. It meant nothing to the rest of us, but Jeffrey jumped to his feet immediately and embraced her with delight.

Needless to say, when Jerry Ewen, president of Playfair Canada, started doing a *Tyrannosaurus rex* imitation, my suspicions about the identity of my own Secret Pal were clearly confirmed.

Once a Week: Fifty-Two Ways to Have Fun on the Job

---

31 | EXPECT THE UNEXPECTED

If you give your employees permission to "throw their inhibitions to the wind" like Gordon Segal did at Crate and Barrel, expect the unexpected. Sure, you give up some measure of daily control, but the rewards may be well worth it. If you can stand the uncertainty that comes with empowering your employees to make their own decisions, you are likely to be pleasantly surprised by the results.

One day Amy Miller, CEO of the seven-store chain of Amy's Ice Cream shops in Austin, Texas, was having a late dinner in a restaurant when she overheard a couple at the next table say, "We'd better hurry up, so we can get to Amy's Ice Cream while there's still time to get locked in." Delighted to hear them talking about her store, but puzzled as to what they meant, Amy quickly finished her own dinner and followed the couple to the nearby Amy's location.

There she discovered that her employees had developed a unique solution to the problem of customers who arrive just as the store is closing and demand service. Often the employees, who are anxious to clean up and get home, view these last-minute customers as a nuisance, and serve them grudgingly, if at all. But the Amy's employees had developed a scheme to turn this problem around. Every Wednesday night, they declared, was "lock-in night." Any customers still in the store on Wednesday night past closing time were locked in and were not allowed to leave the shop until they learned to do the "Time Warp" dance from *The Rocky Horror Picture Show*.

As Amy looked on in amazement, she saw her employees and customers dancing together, following the example of a couple of employees who were demonstrating the steps from on top of the ice cream coolers. Amy later learned that as news of the Wednesday night lock-in had spread through the community, customers like the ones she had overheard talking in the restaurant would plan to arrive at the shop at midnight on purpose, just so they could get locked in and participate in the fun.

"We know that ice cream can definitely cheer up a customer who has had a hard day," says Amy Miller, "so on other nights of the week, we give our employees the option of staying open after closing time to serve customers. But if they have to close the doors, our people tell them, 'Make sure you come back at this time on Wednesday night, and we'll entertain you!' "

Amy Miller knew nothing of the goings-on at her store before that night, but she wholeheartedly approved, since employees and customers dancing together fit in perfectly with the corporate culture she encourages at her stores. "Serving ice cream is an opportunity to make people happy in a stressful social environment," she says. "If coming to our shops is going to be a fun experience for our customers, it had better be a fun experience for our employees as well!"

Amy Miller wants prospective employees to know about her commitment to fun at work from the moment that they apply to work at the store. As Bob Filipczak, writing in *Training Magazine*, tells it, "At Amy's Ice Cream the frivolity starts with the application process. The application form itself is nothing but an empty paper bag.

" 'Like all good ideas,' says Miller, 'this one came about by mistake. One of the stores had run out of formal application forms, so the manager gave an applicant a paper bag to write on, explaining the information the store required. Before giving it back, the applicant did some creative drawing and folding. A tradition was born.'

"Now at Amy's, all you get is a bag. You're asked to do something creative with it while including at least your name and phone number. Miller remembers one bag that came back attached to a helium balloon, made to look like the basket of a hot-air balloon. The basket had pictures of the applicant's accomplishments, as well as other items that were significant to the person. Another applicant converted the bag into a makeshift aquarium, complete with live goldfish. 'We rarely get all the information we need,' Miller concedes, 'but the company simply picks up the rest of the data it desires during the interview process. Most important,' says Miller, 'the application bag is pretty effective at weeding out applicants who probably wouldn't fit into the company culture anyway.' "

32 ARRANGE AN UGLY TIE/UGLY SHOE CONTEST

Pat Gallaty of General Motors designed an unusual stress release event at company headquarters in Detroit: an Ugly Tie Contest. Contestants were allowed to enter any tie they actually presently owned, but no ties could be purchased just to enter the contest. "We invited a panel of outside experts (customers and suppliers) in to pick the winner (loser?)," says Pat. "After the winner was selected and awarded a gold tie pin, all of the ties were cut up and used to make a huge wall hanging. It's part of the decor now and commemorates our fun."

"Some of the female employees who didn't have access to a tie felt left out, however," reports Pat. So General Motors organized a follow-up event: an ugly shoe contest. "Contestants were told to enter only one shoe. The shoe would not be returned in order to rid the world of ugly shoes. No extra points were awarded for ugly smells."

~~~~~~
Once a Week: Fifty-Two Ways to Have Fun on the Job
~~~~~~

33 | CREATE A "LAUGH-A-DAY" CHALLENGE

Just because management suddenly thinks it's time to have some fun, does not necessarily mean that the employees of an organization will respond enthusiastically. It is important for a manager to first establish a convincing rationale for the benefits of fun at work before asking employees to try something new.

One month, the corporate office of the Bank of America issued a "Laugh-a-Day Challenge" to all its northern California employees. For the entire month of April, the employees were challenged to bring in a different joke or cartoon each day to share with their coworkers. Those employees who successfully completed the challenge by sharing something humorous with their coworkers every day of the month were awarded a corporate challenge T-shirt and given a copy of a self-published book that contained the best jokes, cartoons, and other humorous responses to the challenge.

Not all of the Bank of America employees thought that the Laugh-a-Day Challenge was a good idea. One irate employee wrote a letter to the Bank's "Open Line" service inquiring: "How can the bank, at a time when profits are in serious jeopardy, support—even encourage—employees to abuse corporate resources? In the latest issue of *On Your Behalf,* employees are being encouraged to use (abuse) bank photo copy equipment ('share it with someone around you'), abuse interbranch mail, and waste bank supplies.

"I do not consider myself a stick in the mud, and I enjoy a

joke or cartoon as much as the next person, but for human resources to openly encourage people to spend their work time looking for, and sharing with others, jokes and cartoons, is, in my opinion, a total waste of time and resources. Management should be boosting morale and finding solutions whenever possible, but Human Resources has made their latest campaign the biggest joke of all."

This letter of complaint was forwarded to Daniel C. Rowland, the bank's vice president in charge of compensation and benefits. Daniel Rowland's reply presents an excellent rationale for the intentional use of fun and play in a corporate setting. "The monthly 'Be Your Best' Challenges are no joke," he wrote. "They are specifically designed to help bank profitability by improving employee health, productivity, and morale. . . . In Open Line, you question the benefits of laughing. More and more health research now shows that laughter is one of the best stress releases. And stress is our fastest-growing workers' compensation cost (already $2.6 million). You may also be interested to know that Safeway, in one of their recent employee newsletters, encouraged their people to laugh. They said, 'People who laugh a lot live longer, healthier lives, and recover more quickly from stress-related diseases.'

"Are we succeeding in our Corporate Health Program efforts? Apparently so. Each month, an average of two thousand employees send their coupons and letters to us saying we're helping them to adopt and maintain healthier habits. . . . I hope this helps you understand why we have these programs. They are part of a broad-based effort we are making to contain health and workers' compensation costs while improving employee morale and productivity."

As we have seen earlier, laughter and play are not a panacea for curing disease, but they can definitely help combat stress-related illness at work. For the employees of the Bank of America, "laughing all the way to the bank" became an important component of their Corporate Health Program.

Once a Week: Fifty-Two Ways to Have Fun on the Job

34 | ESTABLISH CASUAL DRESS DAYS

More and more organizations are discovering that a rigid dress code does not necessarily increase productivity—in fact, it may even have the opposite effect, by stifling creativity! If yours is an organization where formal business attire is an everyday requirement, see if you can establish Casual Dress Day on alternate Fridays (or Hawaiian Dress Tuesday, or Suspender Thursday, or any of a number of "dress-down" days once a week, or once a month, for a change of pace).

National Demographics and Lifestyles is a consumer database company based in Denver that has more than five hundred employees worldwide. According to Arthur F. Nolan, marketing communications manager of NDL: "Our company was founded on Halloween, in 1975. Therefore, on Founder's Day it's not uncommon to see one of our sales managers in a full clown outfit, complete with makeup and wig, having an important meeting with a client.

"And you can always tell who is visiting the NDL office on 'Leisure Day,' the Friday of every week in the summer and the last Friday of every month the rest of the year. . . . The visitors are the people in business suits!"

When an organization makes the transition from formal to casual dress, it's helpful to manage the change in incremental stages. The United States Fidelity and Guarantee Insurance Company in Baltimore, Maryland, recently designated the last Friday of every month as casual dress day for the five hundred employees of its Information Services Department. Tom Lewis, chief information officer of the corporation, had asked a team working on an essential project what kind of reward would appropriately recognize the successful completion of the job. The overwhelming response was, "Casual dress for a month!," and Tom began to understand the depth of his employees' desire to eliminate formal dress regulations in the department.

After Norm Blake, CEO of USF&G, agreed to let that division be the first of the corporation's six thousand employees to adopt casual dress as an everyday standard, Norm and Tom decided to announce the change in a dramatic fashion. Standing at the front of the room at an all-employee meeting, Norm walked over to Tom, pulled out a large pair of scissors, cut Tom's tie in half, and jubilantly announced, "From this day forward, this division will have casual dress every day!" This announcement was met by a tremendous round of applause from the assembled employees.

When Tom Lewis, smiling, with the stub of his tie hanging down from around his neck, said to the group, "We believe that professionalism is not dictated by the way you dress!" he received a standing ovation. Tom then shared a parable with the group. "Once there were two farmers who were great friends, until one of them got a magnificent cow. The farmer without the cow became resentful and jealous of his neighbor's good fortune. Although he remained civil to his neighbor, inside he was envious. One day, while he was plowing his field, he unearthed a magic lantern. He rubbed the lantern and a

Genie appeared. 'You can have anything your heart desires,' the Genie told the farmer. 'Think deeply, and whatever you wish for will be yours.' The farmer instantly replied, 'Kill my neighbor's cow!'

"We're being given a gift by this company today—we're the first division to have casual dress. If it goes well with us, then maybe the other divisions in the company will have casual dress too, someday. But first, we have to be responsible about it. When you have meetings involving other divisions or involving outside customers, dress the way they dress. Don't flaunt the fact that we've been given a special privilege. It's human nature for those who are envious to want to 'kill the cow.' We want to inspire the other divisions to work for what we have; we don't want to make them resentful."

Something as simple as casual dress can provoke strong reactions from your colleagues, even if they don't mention it to you. A style of informal dress that will be common to the workplace in the next century may provoke outrage and cries of "unprofessionalism" in your organization this year. Remember, the transition from formal to casual dress will have to happen slowly. Manage the change carefully and sensitively.

Once a Week: Fifty-Two Ways to Have Fun on the Job

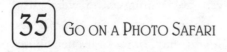 GO ON A PHOTO SAFARI

One of Playfair's clients, Arrow Electronics, recently held its off-site management meeting at a beachfront resort hotel in San

Diego. Playfair trainer Jordan Chouljian devised a unique Photo Safari for the group based on their oceanside location. The group was divided into teams and let loose for the afternoon. Each team was armed with a set of Photo Safari instructions and a disposable underwater camera.

The camera is used to document the fact that the team has successfully solved the various challenges listed on the Photo Safari instruction sheet. At the end of the afternoon, each team brings its camera into a one-hour photo shop and has the pictures developed.

Back in the meeting room, the finished photos are mounted on a wall. Then, in a high-spirited, hilarious evening session, the various teams present their Photo Safari solutions, using their photographic display as a visual aid to chronicle their afternoon adventures.

The beauty of the Photo Safari is that it can be modified and customized to a particular location, or a particular group of people. It is a wonderful way for the members of a team to cooperate and work together in a casual, fun-filled situation. Not only does the group get to explore the unfamiliar environment of the retreat setting, but it is also challenged to use ingenuity, creativity, and risk-taking skills to successfully complete the tasks.

Here is the text of the Photo Safari Jordan created for the Arrow Electronics management team:

- "Boogie Boards" were invented by San Diegan Tom Morrey back in 1970. Take a picture of one of your team members riding a wave on one of these ingenious creations.
- Remember what she sells by the seashore? If so, get a photo of one, preferably without the animal living in it!

- The prevailing habitat found on the bay side of the Silver Strand State Beach is referred to as Salt Marsh. Capture on film any one of the following plants indigenous to a Salt Marsh community. (*Hint:* Be on the lookout for signs!): (1) Pickleweed, (2) Saltword, (3) Alkali Heath.
- Plants of the ocean are frequently used in common household products. Which one plant is used in such things as ice cream, beauty products, and shampoo?
- Arrow Electronics has a highly diversified customer base. Take a picture of your entire team "courting" a potential customer.
- The largest employer in San Diego is the U.S. Navy. Snap a photo of one of its uniformed employees on film. Bonus points for a local Navy SEAL, rumored to be plentiful on Coronado island.
- Underwater cameras have been around for years, but their hefty price tag has prevented most common folk from purchasing them. Now that you've got a disposable one, put that camera to use by taking a picture of your *entire* team UNDERWATER!
- Wildlife is plentiful at the Silver Strand State Beach. First find an animal with two legs, then one with four legs, then one with eight legs!
- In business, sharing resources (otherwise known as *networking*) is a valuable practice. Get a shot of the business card of someone who might be a valuable contact for Arrow Electronics.
- Studies show that when reading newspapers, most professionals seldom read past headlines. Take a picture of a newspaper headline whose story could greatly affect business at Arrow Electronics.
- Is it a passing fad, or a sport that's here to stay? Regard-

less, rollerblading continues to be the hottest new action sport of the nineties. Take a picture of one of your teammates with a person on rollerblades!

- Every city needs an engineering feat of its own. Snap a photo of the only "Aquatic Expansion" bridge in North America, with your teammates in the foreground.
- San Diego has hosted the oldest, most prestigious sailboat race in modern history: The America's Cup. With your teammates in the foreground, get a shot of a racing boat, or the closest rendition you can find.
- The largest navy fleet on the west coast exists in San Diego. Shoot one of the many ships belonging to the fleet on film, with your teammates in foreground.
- Centuries ago, Native American tribes flourished in the Coronado area. Take a picture of something used in ceremonial Native American headdresses and also used in fountain pens in days of old.
- The beach on which you stand has seen some violent storms in recent history, many of which originated south of the border in Baja California, Mexico. Photograph something that may have been washed up on the beach by one of those storms or by a large wave.
- Marine life is also plentiful in the immediate area. Capture a fish on film . . . in any form.
- Toyota's "Oh What a Feeling" commercials proved to be one of the most successful ad campaigns in modern history. Have a picture taken of your entire team doing an Arrow Electronics version of the same commercial. Remember, everyone's feet must be in the air and enthusiasm counts!

36 | SET UP A MAGIC HOTLINE

Suppose someone in your organization develops a better way of doing business. How do you share that information with the rest of your employees in the far-flung reaches of the corporate empire? Supercuts, the national haircutting franchise with more than one thousand stores, developed the "Magic Hotline," a weekly forum for its managers to share with one another their best ideas. (MAGIC was an acronym for the Supercuts' vision statement: "Mastery, Affordability, Graciousness, Inspired, Convenient and Clean.")

Each week a panel in the home office would review the suggestions from the Magic Hotline, and pick the "Idea of the Week." That suggestion would then be recorded on a special telephone line, so the other managers could call up and hear that week's winning idea. The manager who had suggested the winning idea would be credited on the recording, in addition to receiving an award certificate for display in the shop and a Sony Walkman.

Here are some suggestions from the Supercuts Magic Hotline. Can you adapt any of the core concepts to fit your workplace?

- Supercuts does not accept reservations, so sometimes customers have a long wait. Kerry Bevin of San Diego decided to address this "War on Wait." When the wait for a haircut is longer than 45 minutes, Kerry has all the customers in the waiting area place their names into a raffle. The winner gets the service he or she requested (like a haircut, or a haircut and styling) that day for free.

- Sharon Welch's store is located in Joliet, Illinois, a town with legalized river gambling. This inspired Sharon to create a game called "Rolling for Rebates" for her customers in the waiting area. Sharon's store motto is, "If there's a wait, don't hesitate to test your fate and get a rebate." Customers roll a pair of dice: for a 2 they win a free Supercut; a 7 will get them $1 off their next Supercut; and a 12 gets them $2 off their next Supercut. In many cases, friends of customers have had so much fun playing the game that they decided to stay and have their hair cut. Sharon's store has increased its business by ten haircuts per day since she created this game.

- Karen LaRue of Nashville, Tennessee, created buttons for all the hair stylists in the Nashville region to wear. The buttons read, "If I do not recommend a product to you, your haircut will be free." Karen felt that this strategy would stimulate discussion between customers and stylists about the various hair-care products that were available. In the first two months after she introduced the buttons there was an immediate increase of 20 percent in product sales.

- Gail Hereda of Fort Lee, New Jersey, divided her staff into teams, each with a team captain. Every time an employee makes a product sale, the team captain places a sticker in the shape of an ant on the team banner. Gail's slogan is, "The ant takes away the food." So she buys a free lunch for the team with the most ants at the end of the week.

- Kevin Jackson of Green Acres, Florida, offers a discount

to any customer who brings in a can of food. Kevin's shop donates the cans of food to the nearby homeless shelter.

- At her monthly staff meeting, Maria Cajina of San Diego, California, asks employees to stand up and share some things that went well for them that month. Afterward, the Employee of the Month is announced, and each staff member, in turn, gives that person some positive feedback about why he or she deserves the award.

- Whenever Kelly McKenzie of Glendale, Arizona, gets a new trainee in her store, she buys a coffee mug, paints the new trainee's name on it, and fills it with candy. As soon as the trainee graduates from the Hairstylists' Academy, the whole office presents the mug to the new stylist in a "welcome to the store" graduation ceremony.

- Terry Leonard of Los Angeles, California, gives the top-producing employees in the stores he supervises a chance to be "Manager for a Day." The winning employee gets to be store manager on Saturday, when the store is extremely busy, and is given total managerial control of the shop for a day. This process, explains Terry, begins to groom a new generation of managers. It also gives the staff an increased sense of respect for the actual store manager, as employees experience firsthand how involved the manager's job can be.

- On a day when the store is particularly understaffed and under pressure, Kim Gibialante of Greer, South Carolina, holds a spontaneous "Stylist Appreciation Day." Kim sends flowers during the day to an unsuspecting stylist, brings her lunch from the restaurant of her choice, and "makes a big deal of her all day long."

Once a Week: Fifty-Two Ways to Have Fun on the Job

37 | DESIGN STRESS SUPPORT KITS

A sales manager at Dun and Bradstreet Software noticed that the phone consultants who reported to her were under a great deal of stress. "They're on the firing line with our customers every day," she said. "The people calling in for help are almost always under pressure, so it's crucial for our consultants to stay calm if we're going to develop a positive, long-term relationship with our customers." To help the consultants keep their cool, she created a "Stress Support Kit" that included chewing gum, aspirin, a comedy cassette, wind-up toys for the desktop, and a rubber head for squeezing during tense moments on the phone.

Playfair's Ritch Davidson was so taken with the idea that he created a similar collection for his own clients and coworkers. This "Playfair Stress Support Kit" contains three "vegetable pens" (a pen in the shape of a carrot, a corncob pen, and a pickle pen), a set of wind-up chattering teeth with little moving feet, a red foam clown nose, and an audiocassette by the Playfair staff called "Laugh Your Stress Away."

The label that Ritch designed for the kit reads:

If you're taking yourself too seriously, it's time to lighten up already!

Indications: For the temporary relief of clenched teeth, tight necks and muscles, hair about to be pulled out by the roots, and general cranky behavior—all associated with the common stressors at work, at home, in traffic, on the golf course, in long lines . . .

Dosage: Use as often as needed at the first signs of discomfort.

The vegetable pens are to ease the pain the next time you have to write a check with more than two zeroes in it. *The chattering teeth* are for the next time you're stuck on a call with an unbelievably boring client . . . Let the teeth walk across your desk. *The clown nose* is for you to put on the next time you are stuck in a traffic jam: it won't do you much good, but the drivers of the other cars around you will go wild! And finally, the audiocassette, *"Laugh Your Stress Away,"* will help you see that in any stressful situation there is always another way to look at the situation that can help to put it into perspective. *Why choose stress?*

Is there anyone in your office who will be pressed to meet a demanding project deadline in the next few weeks? Take a trip to the toystore and design your own customized "Contents Under Pressure" stress support kit for him or her. It doesn't matter if your style is to present the stress support kit with great ceremony, or to leave it hidden somewhere, to be discovered as an anonymous gift. What's important is that during a time of tension and stress, the person knows that someone is thinking about him. As psychotherapist Annette Goodheart, the author of *Laughter Therapy,* has so eloquently stated, "Just because we're miserable doesn't mean we can't laugh about it!"

38 | ORCHESTRATE A MONTHLY OUTING

The Self-Esteem Seminars Company in Pacific Palisades, California, orchestrates a monthly outing for its staff members and invited guests, as a way of getting to know one another outside of the normal work routine. Responsibility for planning the event rotates each month among the various staff members; the company-wide celebrations have taken the form of a beach party, a visit to a comedy club, a night of driving midget race cars, and a broom ball competition at the local ice skating rink.

Jack Canfield, the company president and coauthor of the best-selling book *Chicken Soup for the Soul,* reports that the regularity of the meetings is the key to making them happen. "If we just left them up to chance," he says, "something 'more important' would always come up. But it's a regular part of our schedule, everybody puts it down in his or her calendar, and one specific individual is always in charge of making it happen. This way, we never miss a month of organized fun together!"

39 | LOOK FOR THE INNER CHILD

Eldon Peterson, vice president of sales for the VHA Supply Company in Irving, Texas, made up campaign-sized buttons with the baby picture of each member of his sales staff. He also asked each salesperson for "one true fact about yourself that no one else in the company knows," and attached those "fact sheets" to the appropriate buttons. At the VHA Supply Company national sales meeting, Eldon randomly distributed the buttons to his sales force with the instruction to "give this to the person to whom it belongs."

The members of the sales staff then walked around the meeting room asking one another questions like, "Are you the person who burned down the pasture while playing with dynamite when you were twelve years old?" or "Were you the prom queen in 1978?" Not only was it a fun way for his salespeople to get to know one another, said Eldon, it also gave them practice in asking the kind of probing questions that would be helpful to them in their jobs.

Once a Week: Fifty-Two Ways to Have Fun on the Job

40 REVERSE THE ROLES

Once a year, the executives of station KHET-TV in Honolulu throw a party for the rest of the staff. "It's our way of showing appreciation for the people who take care of us all year," says Dr. James Young, who is the executive director of Hawaii Public Television. "So this is a party where we serve them— the management executives buy, cook, and serve all the food to the support staff."

Kasey Dorn and Debbie White, the Houston area general managers for Supercuts, took the role-reversal concept even a step further. "August is our busiest month," recalls Kasey Dorn. "So we set lofty goals for the month with the sixteen shops in the Houston area, and we told them if they met their goals, we would show up at the shops and be their 'servants' for a day."

The next month, Kasey and Debbie spent a day at each of the seven shops that had exceeded their goals for August. Kasey and Debbie arrived in French maid outfits, complete with little white lace hats and aprons that said, "Supercuts Servants for the Day." Kasey recalls that, "We told them that we would do anything except cut hair and take money. We gave each of the hair stylists a little bell that they could ring whenever they wanted us to do something for them. They had us running around sweeping the floor, wetting hair, giving shampoos, picking up dropped combs. We took down the names of the customers who were waiting for a haircut, we took orders for lunch, we went to pick up lunch, we went out to the parking lot to retrieve things the stylists had left in their cars . . .

"The whole thing gave us a chance to interact with the stylists in a fun way, and to show them that we're real people, not just managers. They got to see that we understand what it's like for them to be out on the floor every day, that we understand what their jobs are really like. And it gave us a fun, informal way to interact with the customers, to talk to them about their perceptions of how we do business. As they were leaving, most of the customers were saying, 'Wow, I can't believe this. I can't wait to tell my boss about this!' "

CHAPTER 7

Rituals and Celebrations

I once heard Thich Nhat Hanh speak about the concept of "Sangha." A Sangha is a group of people who gather together with a common purpose, a common mission, either to worship together, to create a product, or to perform a service together. Those are the practical reasons for a Sangha. But the spiritual purpose of a Sangha is to help the members of the group become more aware of their connections with each other and with the larger world.

As I listened to Thich Nhat Hanh speak, I realized that the people in Playfair could be a "Sangha," that we could become even more of a team than we were already. Even though most of us are separated by great geographical distances, and even though we are constantly traveling, we could still feel a deep sense of connection with each other. A Sangha is the ultimate form of team building, because the Sangha members don't just think of themselves as separate entities, they think of themselves as a part of a larger whole.

Thich Nhat Hanh used a metaphor that day that has always

stayed with me. He said, "You are not in isolation; you are a limb of a body—the Sangha body." Obviously, the parts of a body need to work together if the body is going to operate successfully in the world. For example, it makes no sense for the arm to be jealous of the leg. They are both more than just "arm" or "leg"—together, they are part of a larger "body," and together they are more powerful, more functional, more useful than they are as separate limbs.

I wanted to tell the Playfair staff members that our Playfair organization was like a body in that way. That we are part of something bigger than our separate selves. That we are a part of a team. Part of a Sangha.

Having a community at work, a community of people that care about each other, that nourish each other and support each other, is one of the most important goals for me in business. Of course, it's important that we're profitable, and of course it's important that we're doing work that makes me proud. But it is of utmost importance to me that the people in Playfair enjoy a sense of supportive community with each other.

A sense of community develops in an organization as the members of a company discover a sense of shared history. Let's think of shared history as a series of events that define the internal culture of an organization—occasions the participants will talk about and refer to, long after the events themselves are over. Some of this shared history evolves naturally over time, in the course of doing business together. But a sense of shared history can also be deliberately facilitated by a manager who is willing to introduce some non–business-related team-building experiences into the mix of corporate life. We have already looked at several successful examples: Kirt Womack's paper airplane flying contest, his volleyball game on the factory floor . . . the monthly outings of Jack Canfield's Self-Esteem company . . . Dr. Jeff Alexander's trip to the shopping mall with his staff. In each of these situations, the employees can look back at a shared experience and feel a sense of accomplishment, or a sense of strength, or a sense of closeness as a result of fun shared as a group.

In the Playfair organization, most of our shared history has its roots in our annual staff re-treat. The members of the Playfair organization are located all over the United States and Canada, and we only get together as an entire group once a year. For a long time I had referred to our annual company off-site meeting as "The Playfair Retreat." Then someone pointed out to me that to "retreat" means to move backward, which was certainly not the image I wanted to project. But what else would we call it? "The Playfair Advance" sounded ridiculous. Then Ritch Davidson, one of the senior staff members, came up with the spelling "re-treat," which solved our problem nicely. It set up exactly the expectation I wanted the staff members to have: that they were in for another five-day treat!

Our re-treats typically take place at a ranch we rent, which has cabins for sleeping and a large hall for meetings. There's a breathtaking view of the night sky at the ranch, which only adds to the wonderful feeling I get when I walk through the grounds and see two people who were complete strangers before I recruited them for the company lost in a deep conversation. I'm filled with a sense of accomplishment and a sense of belonging to something much bigger than myself.

During the Playfair re-treat we intentionally create a variety of history-making events. We've done a ropes course together, taken a self-defense class, and an African drumming class. We've steeped in the volcanic mud baths at Calistoga, participated in a clowning workshop, and attended a wedding together. We've camped out together and hiked among the

redwoods. We've gone to Sanibel Island in Florida for a computer training re-treat ("Nerds in Paradise"), traveled to British
Columbia together for a re-treat in the snow-capped moun-
tains, and brought the entire company together for a winter
re-treat in Aruba. For our twentieth anniversary of the company, we published a commemorative wall calendar that featured scores of different photos spanning twenty years of our
adventures together.

In addition to our group adventures, an important source
of shared history has been the rituals and celebrations that are a
major part of our corporate culture. I am a great believer in
taking time out to celebrate your successes—the small ones as
well as the large ones. The first day of our staff re-treat is always
filled with ongoing rituals that have become a tradition with us:
an opening ceremony where everyone in the company receives
a flood of positive feedback; a welcoming celebration for the
new employees; ceremonies for important service anniversaries
(such as ten years with the company); and the presentation of a
commemorative gift for everyone in attendance.

I am always on the lookout for souvenir gifts to commem-
orate each re-treat. One year we purchased watches with the
Playfair logo on them as our commemorative gift. The watches
had been the brainchild of Playfair staff trainer Mahara Brenna;
Charmaine Silverstein, my executive assistant, oversaw their
design and purchase, so I asked Mahara and Charmaine to develop a ceremony for presenting the watches to the staff. I was
just as surprised as the rest of the group when the two of them
arrived costumed as Father and Mother Time. Mahara wore a
skullcap over her hair that made her appear bald, sported a fake
mustache and beard, and carried a long staff. Charmaine wore a
powdered white wig to cover her hair and a baggy dress stuffed
with pillows. She carried a large wicker basket full of watches.

"What time is it?" they asked each other, looking worried. And then they proceeded to answer their own question.

"Time flies!"

"No time like the present!"

"No present like the time!"

"It must be . . . PLAYFAIR TIME!"

They distributed the watches with instructions for each of us to fasten a watch on the wrist of the person next to us. Then Father and Mother Time retreated from the room to a chorus of cheers, whistles, and enthusiastic hand clapping and foot stomping.

The following year, when it was time to distribute the commemorative Playfair beach towels, Father and Mother Time returned, back by popular demand, and the reception was even more enthusiastic than the year before. From that time on, no Playfair re-treat would be complete without a guest appearance by Father and Mother Time. Such is a way company traditions are born.

Most of Playfair's company-wide ceremonies have been planned well in advance, but sometimes celebrations will erupt spontaneously, like the Blessing Way, which occurred when Carla revealed that she was engaged; the spontaneous Graduation Ceremony, which came about when Sarah announced she had received her master's degree; and the Fertility Ritual, conducted by the women for Terry after her wedding (it worked —she gave birth to a baby girl!).

These ongoing rituals and ceremonies add playfulness, drama, and excitement to our meetings. While they certainly make the meetings more fun, they serve a deeper purpose as well. During the time of our rituals and celebrations we speak a different kind of language with each other than we normally speak, and this nonverbal communication helps forge a bond that is an essential part of building a team. The rituals that are repeated year after year give a familiar structure to our meetings, and they help us address on a group level common concerns of identity, connectedness, and power.

In the middle of the staff re-treat one summer, I looked around and knew with absolute certainty that there was no-where else on earth I would rather be. I knew those days would be five of the most wonderful days of the year for me, that no matter what—and I knew there would be times of conflict along with the joy—the overriding feeling would be one of excitement, support, and Sangha.

I tried to express to the Playfair staff how important these summer re-treats were to me, and how important it was to have them in my life. I told them I was very proud of the work that we were doing together. And then I found myself admitting something pretty amazing. I said, "In my heart of hearts, I don't know whether the purpose of going away together on re-treat is to prepare us to be successful and profitable for the rest of the year, or if the purpose of this company is to be successful and profitable, so we can afford to go away together every year!"

When you take your company, department, or team away, things can happen to strengthen the emotional well-being of your organization in ways that rarely occur during the normal workday or workweek. At a retreat location, there is a relaxed atmosphere, and a natural, easy focus on team building. Once you are away from the everyday pressures and distractions of the office, your group has the opportunity to focus on clarifying a vision of your organizational future, and on bonding emotion-ally. When you take your organization to a re-treat location, you create a fertile setting for rituals and celebrations to occur spontaneously. You greatly increase the opportunity for shared history—a history that can have a positive impact on your work together for many years to come.

41 | DESIGN COMPANY LOGO ITEMS

At every Playfair staff re-treat we have a ceremonial presentation of an article of clothing featuring the Playfair logo. Each time, performing the ceremony has made receiving the jacket, T-shirt, or beach towel that much more meaningful. Whenever I put on my Playfair baseball cap in the years since I received it, I remember the ceremony during which it was presented.

I once gave a talk to a group of salespeople from MCI who were meeting at a resort hotel in Phoenix. When I returned to my hotel room after the talk, I found a pair of sunglasses with the MCI logo on the lenses waiting for me on my bed. (I later found out that the meeting planner had left these sunglasses in all the participants' rooms.) I put on the sunglasses, looked in the mirror, saw my face through the MCI logo, and thought, "What fun! What a great idea!"

I immediately decided to have sunglasses made up with the Playfair logo, in time for our annual summer staff re-treat. But the idea of leaving the sunglasses on the pillows of the Playfair participants did not appeal to me. I knew the glasses would make a much greater impression if we all discovered them to-gether.

The re-treat was held at our favorite location, Rainbow

Ranch in Calistoga, California. On the second day of the re-treat, the entire company gathered in the lodge for our morning meeting. After we had been working steadily for two hours, we needed a break. I led the group outdoors and we arranged ourselves in a large circle. Then I asked them to close their eyes and to start chanting, "The future's so bright, we're gonna need shades!" Meanwhile, my assistant and I walked around inside the circle and placed the sunglasses over each person's closed eyes.

As the Playfair staff members opened their eyes, I could see broad grins of delight on their faces. The chant, "The future's so bright, we're gonna need shades!" suddenly doubled in volume. In fact, that chant resurfaced many times during the five days of the re-treat, and it soon became an ongoing chorus of celebration anytime anything positive happened in the company.

Distributing the sunglasses to the group was a demonstration of my appreciation for the work we had done together as a team. If you're looking to express appreciation to your team, it must happen in a public ceremony, rather than privately. And public ceremonies are more fun and more memorable if they contain some element of surprise, some element of "theater" about them.

Over the years, some of the ceremonies that have accompanied the presentation of Playfair logo items have been long and elaborate; others were over in only a few brief minutes. Some of the ceremonies generated peals of laughter; others were quite emotional. To me, personally, the ritual that accompanied the presentation of the Playfair jackets was the most moving of all. As each staff member received his or her jacket, he or she also received a flood of positive feedback from the other members of the company. One by one, each of us who received a jacket stood in the middle of the circle, with the jacket draped

over our shoulders, while the rest of the staff called out, voicing
their feelings of support and appreciation for us. Then the person in the middle of the circle reached into the basket, pulled
out another jacket, and read off the name embroidered on it—
then that person would take her place in the center. It took
most of the afternoon to give out all of the jackets, but it was a
wonderful afternoon, filled with laughter, tears, and open-
hearted appreciation.

As a manager, you can delegate the brainstorming of these
kinds of activities to individuals on your staff who have a creative imagination and a flair for the dramatic. After all, it's not
as if I invented all of the Playfair rituals myself—far from it.
After the first few, I delegated the responsibility to others, to
encourage their creative thinking. That way I could be as surprised as everyone else when the presentations took place. At
one re-treat I gave Carol Ann and Mahara a supply of Playfair
logo pens and asked them to figure out some way to present
them to the group. The two of them set up a flip chart in the
front of the meeting room and announced, "You're going to
need to take some notes on this presentation." Before any of us
could reach for our pens, they told us, "And you can find some
writing implements at . . ."

At this point they turned to the page on the flip chart on
which was written:

1. A place too cold to grow some mold.
2. A place to meditate and eliminate.
3. A place to communicate and commiserate.
4. A shady place to stuff your face.

For a few moments, we all sat in our chairs and stared at
them blankly, without a clue as to what we were expected to

do. Then, as we realized what the clues meant, we made a mad dash for:

1. The refrigerator
2. The restrooms
3. The pay phones
4. The outdoor picnic tables on which we just had lunch

The first person to reach each of these locations found bowls filled with company logo pens, which he or she handed out to the other staff members. We returned to the meeting room from the four corners of the lodge, energized and ready to take notes with a vengeance.

Once a Week: Fifty-Two Ways to Have Fun on the Job

 42 DISTRIBUTE STUFFED ANIMALS

When Arthur Garza, director of sales for a major hotel chain, describes his management philosophy, he says, "Our jobs are about selling, so I try to make sales fun for my people. When I hire new sales trainees, I take them into my office and show them a wall covered with shelves full of stuffed animals. I tell them, 'Each one of those stuffed animals represents a major sale made over the last few months.' Then I go into my supply box of stuffed animals and I give them each an armful. I say to them, 'These animals belong on this shelf in a place of honor. When you make a sale, I want you to bring one back to me, so we can put it up on the shelf where it belongs!' "

The salespeople also know that it is important to Arthur to take time to celebrate the sale. And since the arrival of a stuffed animal in his office is an obvious sign that it is time to celebrate, the salespeople have taken great pleasure in its delivery. Once, one of his salespeople lowered a stuffed bear from the third floor on a fishing line and swung it through the window in Arthur's office. Another time, Arthur was using the toilet in the men's room when he heard a knock on the door, and a stuffed poodle came flying over the top of the stall and landed in his lap.

Still another time, Arthur was talking on the phone to a longtime supplier, when three of his top sales agents came rushing into his office. They began running around his desk and pelting him with stuffed animals, while they screamed about a major client they had landed. The supplier, having visited Arthur's office and knowing all about his wall of stuffed animals, started cheering along with them. "We live to make sales and we love to make sales," said Arthur, "so we might as well make a party out of it!"

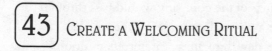

Once a Week: Fifty-Two Ways to Have Fun on the Job

43 | CREATE A WELCOMING RITUAL

Instead of waiting until someone retires to have a party, why not throw a party for someone's first day at work? What a great

way to give a new employee an immediate sense of being part
of the team, and to say "Welcome. We're glad you're here."

In the Playfair organization, we send employees flowers
on their first day at work, and hold an elaborate "welcoming
ceremony" at the first staff re-treat they attend. The prototype
for the welcoming ceremony was "Eddie DeAngelo and the
Circle of Secrets." Ten years ago, when we thought about what
it meant to have a new trainee entering the company, we asked
ourselves, "How can we empower our newest member to feel
like a part of the group?" Playfair trainer Mahara Brenna came
up with a novel solution: a ritual to make Eddie, who at that
time was the new trainee, the "Keeper of Secrets."

There are bits of history, politics, and secrets about any
organization that a newcomer can only learn over time. Because
a newcomer is not privy to this information, he naturally feels
disempowered. The opposite of power is vulnerability, so one
way to even the balance of power was for the rest of us to make
ourselves vulnerable to Eddie by giving him some "superhuman
power" over us.

Under Mahara's direction, the members of the company
arranged themselves in a large circle around which Eddie was
led, blindfolded, from one person to the next. Each person
whispered to him one true fact about himself or herself that no
one else in the company knew. A roll of crepe paper marked
the route of Eddie's journey, so that over the next few days,
whenever the members of the company would pass through the
area, they would see a physical reminder of the ritual.

By placing the new hire in a "preferred position," and
by sharing ourselves with him, the members of the Playfair
organization extended an extraordinary welcome to the newcomer in our midst. This tradition has continued for many
years, and continues to live in our memories for years afterward.

All of the subsequent Playfair welcoming rituals have contained the same basic elements of the Circle of Secrets: to celebrate the newcomer's arrival in a playful way, and to make a gesture of accommodation and equality that says, "You are a valuable member of this team. You may be new here, but you're not alone. There is a lot of support for you here. We welcome you. This is a safe place to play!"

Once a Week: Fifty-Two Ways to Have Fun on the Job

44 CREATE AN OATH OF OFFICE

When the president of the United States assumes power, he takes an oath of office that delineates his mission and his responsibility to his constituents. What if you designed an oath of office for your organization, to give the new hires a sense of the history and the mission of your company? You can have some fun with it, like Len LaBella, the president of Santa Monica Hospital in Los Angeles, did.

In 1989, the hospital was expanding and had hired fifteen new managers to meet its growing needs. The new managers had only been working at the hospital for a few months when Len called a meeting to welcome these new members of his management team. Halfway through the meeting Len disappeared, and soon reappeared dressed up in a makeshift hippopotamus outfit.

This normally dignified, sane CEO was wearing hippo ears and a body-length hippo cloak, and carrying a wand with a hippo doll attached at the end of it. With a wave of his wand, the ceremony began. Len briefly explained that the hippo symbolized the qualities of a "High-Performance Organization" (HPO) and a High-Performance Manager. He then proceeded to read the official "HPO-cratic Oath" from a scroll:

> **Whereas,** the high-performance manager, like the hippo, has the metaphysical stature to carry any workload, yet the deftness of foot to tiptoe through the most challenging quagmire of governmental and professional regulations, and
>
> **Whereas,** the hippo and its high-performance counterparts personify the ideals of shared values, quality, integrity, respect for all those with whom they come into contact, and
>
> **Whereas,** the hippo symbolizes the essence of the corporate manager whose expansive capabilities include a heart bigger than an autoclave and ears that constantly scan the environment for new and innovative ideas, and
>
> **Whereas** the hippo, like the corporate middle manager, has prospered and endured for centuries disproving the endangered species theory expounded by anthropologists and big city business editors, and
>
> **Whereas,** the hippo, and its friends the corporate managers, emit a strong and sure culture
>
> **Now,** therefore, I realize that the hippo is my hero, and I do here, today, affirm my allegiance and devotion to the hippo and all for which it stands.

Containing their laughter as best as they could, the new initiates repeated each line after Len LaBella. After the closing

line, Len led his new team in a rousing "Hip-hippo-ray!" The
new managers were given a gift package containing a sweatshirt,
T-shirt, and watch, all embossed with the hippo logo. They also
received a supply of "hippo-gram" notepads for sending one
another notes.

The result of all this ritualized silliness? According to Len
LaBella, in addition to bringing official closure to the orientation period at the hospital, the hippo ritual builds teamwork,
solidifies camaraderie, creates excitement and anticipation
among managers about to enter the HPO program, and rein-
forces high performance as a value of the organization in a
lighthearted way. "Not a bad payoff for periodically making a
fool out of myself," he says.

Once a Week: Fifty-Two Ways to Have Fun on the Job

---

45 | GIVE SOME MONEY AWAY

Luke Barber, my friend who arranged the surprise picnic in the
parking garage, is a faculty member in the philosophy department at Richland College in Dallas. Almost every Friday afternoon, a group of faculty members and staff from the college
meet at a local bar for happy hour to finish off the workweek.

If you've ever gathered with a group of colleagues for
drinks after work, you're probably aware of the fact that the last
people to leave are always the ones who get stuck with the bill.
One Friday, people had, of course, been leaving throughout the
evening, and, as was the custom, had each tossed some money

on the table. The evening ended, and Luke was left at the table with two of the women from the counseling center. The three of them prepared to call it a night and head their separate ways.

"What usually happens in such a situation," recounts Luke, "is that the check comes and you count up the amount of money that everyone has left on the table, and you are about $5 short. But that's okay, you are really feeling good after killing off a couple of pitchers of beer, so you feel fine about the $5 deficit. After all, what's $5 or $10 between friends?"

However, something happened that particular Friday that had never happened to Luke and his coworkers before. After everyone had left, the three actually had $12 too much, even after they had given a substantial tip to the waitress. So they began to discuss what they would do with the $12. The most logical suggestion was to start happy hour the next week with $12 in the kitty.

"But then foggier heads prevailed, and the three of us decided to do something wacky with the money," recalls Luke. "We decided to give the $12 away." They looked around the bar and each of them picked out people they wanted to meet. Then they got up, one at a time, with a few dollars from the kitty in hand. They walked over to the stranger, put the money down in front of him or her, and said, "Here, I'd like for you to have this money." Then they walked back to their table and sat down.

Much to their amazement, Luke and his cohorts found it impossible to get rid of the excess money, however hard they tried. In fact, within fifteen minutes they had $26 in front of them. People had begun coming over to their table to give them their money back—and saying, "Here's your $2 back, and I'll raise you $2!" Before it was over there were people yelling to each other from across the room, things like, "I'll give you $10 and trade you two of the men at our table for two of the women at yours!" Patrons were furiously and randomly handing money to each other, back and forth and all around the bar.

"It was an amazing experience," Luke remembers, "one of those rare occasions where one crazy, spontaneous act of giving brought a bunch of total strangers together. Regardless of our obvious differences and similarities, there we were, sharing with each other like old friends."

Most people are very serious about money, which makes it a powerful way of getting people's attention. As Dr. Jeff Alexander found out at the shopping mall, as the Playfair staff members found out at the tollbooth, and as Luke Barber and his colleagues found out at Happy Hour, if you combine fun with a little cash, you can bring some unexpected delight to the people around you. Give some money away where it's least expected, and see what can happen.

Once a Week: Fifty-Two Ways to Have Fun on the Job

46 | PUT A NEW SPIN ON THE HOLIDAY GIFT EXCHANGE

Exchanging holiday gifts in the office is one activity that can bring as much angst as joy to both gift giver and receiver. How do you ensure that everyone gets a gift of equal value? You can always set a price limit of $15. How do you ensure that everyone gets a gift? You could put all the gifts in a grab bag and let people pull out their gifts randomly. Or you could have everyone put their name in a hat in advance, and each giver would pick the name of the person for whom they would buy a gift.

But these rules and regulations lack a certain drama, a certain excitement, a certain . . . chance to play, like you did when you were a child. The holiday gift exchange that has become a tradition at Playfair was first taught to us by Carol Ann Fried. For the give-away, all the participants were instructed to find an item that they already owned but were willing to part with, an item that someone else might enjoy receiving. The participants then wrapped these recycled presents as attractively as possible and brought them to the gift exchange.

Let's go back—in the spirit of the season, like the ghost of Christmas past—to witness the exchange firsthand.

"Would everyone please gather in a circle and put the gift you've brought in the center of the circle?" instructed Carol Ann. "I'm going to pass around this envelope that has slips of paper numbered one to twenty-five in it. Without looking, reach into the envelope and pull out a slip of paper—that paper will determine the order in which you pick your gift.

"Who has number one? Carla. Okay, Carla, you're the first person to play, so right now pick a present and unwrap it." (Carla pounces on her gift and unwraps it. It's a maroon Wreck Beach sweatshirt. She looks momentarily horrified, but gamely models it for the rest of us before returning to her seat.)

"Who has number two? Okay, Louise, you have a choice. You can either pick a present and unwrap it, or you can take Carla's present, and then she'll pick a different one. What do you want to do?" (Louise ponders briefly, looking back and forth from the sweatshirt to the pile of gifts. She makes a sudden dash into the center of the circle, grabs a large rectangular box, and tears at the paper to reveal a briefcase with a clock in the middle of it.)

"Okay, who's next? Marlon, you've got number three? You've

*got even better choices. You can pick a present, or you can take Carla's,
or you can take Louise's, and then she'll pick a new one." (Marlon
doesn't hesitate at all. He picks a present, which turns out to be a
portable clothes steamer.)*

*"Who's next? Sarah, you've got number four. What do you
want to do?" (Sarah gleefully takes the briefcase from Louise.) "Now,
Louise, the rule is that you cannot take the briefcase right back from
Sarah on this turn. But if you get the chance to choose something
again later, you can get your beloved briefcase back again. So . . .
what's it gonna be?"*

*(Louise eyes Marlon suspiciously, then grabs his clothes steamer.
The scene closes with Marlon dancing around the circle, delighted to be
rid of the clothes steamer, then carefully choosing yet another package
from the heap at the center of the circle. . . .)*

As you can see, nothing is safe in our Recycled Holiday
Gift Exchange—and there is a constant ebb and flow of tension
as the most treasured gifts pass from one person to another. The
beauty (and the drama) of the exchange is that once you have
unwrapped a present that you absolutely hate, you are not stuck
with it forever. The trick is to try to convince others (through
your feigned joy and enthusiasm) of the value of your gift, so
they will take it away from you. (Of course, you'll want to
downplay your love for a gift you absolutely adore, since you
know it can be swiped from you at any given moment.)

After about half the gifts have been chosen, and a number
of the participants have received gifts they desperately want to
unload, the Recycled Holiday Gift Exchange starts to sound
like an ancient bazaar, with the merchants shouting out the
virtues of their wares to each successive player. "Hey, Amo,
come over here, this is what you want! Take this, don't even
think about it! Look at this beautiful fondue set—the perfect
anniversary gift for your wife! How can you live without it?"

The first time I played this game with the Playfair staff I was seated next to Playfair facilitator Andy Weisberg. The gift that Andy had unwrapped was an orange ceramic dachshund, whose back contained a hollowed-out space for holding cocktail frankfurters. From the moment Andy opened it, he tried everything he could think of to unload it. He hawked his prize in a Russian accent, in a French accent, in a Yiddish accent. "Look at this pedigreed dog—the perfect gift for your kids. One-of-a-kind sculpture! Anybody looking for a work of art? A priceless work of art! Attention dog lovers—complete your valuable collection of canine memorabilia!" Andy was constantly in motion, waving the dog over his head, making it dance, making it talk, getting down on his hands and knees to beg for a trade . . . any trade.

Of course, you might ask yourself the question, What possible use could anyone find for anything so ugly? What would possibly possess someone to take that pathetic ceramic dachshund off his hands, no matter how much he begged and pleaded? I often ask myself the same question, as I stare across the desk at my ceramic dachshund business card holder.

Once a Week: Fifty-Two Ways to Have Fun on the Job

---

 47 DESIGN PERSONALIZED FORTUNE COOKIES

If you live near a large city, you can probably find a Chinese bakery that will specially bake fortune cookies to include fortunes you design yourself.

Write personalized fortunes containing specific information about the people who will be eating the fortune cookies. Then serve these custom-designed fortune cookies to an unsuspecting staff at a coffee break during a long meeting, or for dessert after a meal. This is an idea that can definitely fit into even the most strained company budget: the cost of twenty-five specially baked fortune cookies in an Oakland, California, Chinese bakery, for example, is only $2!

At a dinner meeting of the twenty-five Playfair staff members, the organizers ordered a box of fresh baked "action fortune cookies," where each cookie contained an action for the recipient to perform. Each of these cookies called for a specific interaction between two of the group members, and each action contained information based on shared personal history, or unique habits or skills. (One fortune, for example, read, "Ask Jerry to teach you how to hang a spoon from your nose," a talent for which Jerry Ewen has long been famous at many company outings.)

Each member of the group randomly picks a fortune cookie from a basket that is passed around, and each person is asked to open her cookie at the same time as everybody else. As soon as we broke open our fortune cookies at the Playfair dinner, there was a moment of stunned silence followed by a rush of energy, as each staff member rushed over to the one person who could complete the task described in his fortune. Of course, that other person was simultaneously running off to fulfill the fortune inside his own cookie, which created complete pandemonium among the group (exactly our intention!). Here is a sampling of the action fortunes from that memorable dinner party:

- Have Charmaine tell you the story of her most memorable train trip.

- Have Mahara teach you an Afro-funk move.
- Find out Miles's favorite recipe (formerly he was a chef!).
- Have Carol Ann demonstrate (using charades) where she gets all her wild earrings.
- Have Carla teach you some of her Brain Gym relaxation techniques.
- Krysta formerly worked as managing editor of *Marriage Magazine*. Let her suggest three romantic things to do on a weekend.
- Ask Katie about her trip to Australia.
- Tell Matt one thing you appreciate about his leadership of this company.
- Have Louise sing you a song that reminds her of you.
- Give Jordan a very special "welcome to the company" greeting of your own design.
- Ask Terry to demonstrate her entry for "America's Funniest Home Videos."
- Ask Andy to show you a performance from his former career as a mime.

Best of all, after the madcap activity dies down, you still have your fortune cookie to eat.

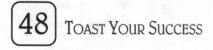

Once a Week: Fifty-Two Ways to Have Fun on the Job

48 | TOAST YOUR SUCCESS

The holiday season is invariably the time when someone in the office will raise a glass of eggnog and propose a toast to the health of the organization. But why wait for that once-a-year office Christmas party to raise a glass to the continuing success of your company? You can extend the giving spirit of the holiday season all year round. Why not pick some random days of the month to have a group celebration? How about creating your own company holidays? Bring some champagne to work a couple times a month, so the members of your department can gather together on a Friday afternoon and publicly celebrate your successes. If your company policy forbids intoxicants, then toasting the achievements of the past two weeks with sparkling apple or grape juice can be a good nonalcoholic substitute—it's not the taste that counts, it's the toast!

Once a Week: Fifty-Two Ways to Have Fun on the Job

 PERSONALIZE YOUR SEASONS GREETINGS

Looking for something different for the company Christmas card? If you have access to a color photocopy machine, you can create an original card from your own photo collection. For the Playfair Seasons Greetings card, Playfair's Vice Emperor Ritch Davidson photographed a bag of frozen peas sitting on a mound of dirt, the sign outside the local Goodwill office, and two screwdriver-like implements. As a guide for our poor, perplexed clients who undoubtedly had trouble figuring out its meaning, Ritch included a translation on the back of the card: "Peas on earth, goodwill two awl."

50 | PRACTICE RANDOM KINDNESS

Just as I was about to begin talking to a joint union–management group of the Tennessee Valley Authority about "Putting Fun to Work," a representative of the facility service department came over to me and asked if I would read an announcement to the group. The announcement read:

If you have any unopened containers of soap, shampoo, lotion, or mouthwash in your hotel room that you would like to donate to the homeless, please bring them to the Facility Service Exhibit. We will collect these items and distribute them to homeless people in the community. Please do not bring towels, lamps, mirrors, beds, or anything else that's bolted down! Thank you.

I was delighted with the announcement, which met with sustained applause from the group when I read it aloud at the beginning of my presentation. I told the group that this was a wonderful example of the concept of practicing random kindness and senseless acts of beauty.

The Playfair staff had been sharing this concept during the past year with students in colleges and universities all over North America. Under the guidance and inspiration of Playfair trainer Carol Ann Fried, the Playfair staff had talked about random kindness at more than three hundred campuses, under the sponsorship of the New Student Orientation programs. This is what we told the new students:

"Sometimes the real world isn't as welcoming or as safe as your college community. We all know about random violence and senseless cruelty in the world and some of us have been touched by it personally.

"A writer in Sausalito, California, named Anne Herbert coined a phrase to get people to focus and act on the opposite idea. PRACTICE RANDOM KINDNESS AND SENSELESS ACTS OF BEAUTY started as an underground movement and recently it's gone mainstream—you can find it on bumper stickers, buttons, and posters. And it's really catching on, because, you see, just as violence begets more violence, so too does kindness beget more kindness.

"Random kindness and senseless acts of beauty can be done on a grand scale or on a small scale. Often it is practiced completely anonymously. Kind acts can be as simple as intro-ducing five people in the cafeteria line to five other people, or being a blood donor, or picking up garbage as you go from class to class. They can be as grandiose as painting a grungy classroom in the dead of night, or collecting clothes with a bunch of friends and delivering them to homeless folks, or calling every-one you care about on Thanksgiving and telling them why you are thankful that they are in your life.

"In just a moment, I'm going to ask you and your group of twelve to practice random kindness and a senseless act of beauty. I'm going to ask you to huddle together and plan one thing that you can do together as a group within the next seven days. When you are ready, send a group spokesperson up to the stage to tell us about your project. Here are a few other exam-ples to get you thinking: leave thank-you notes for maintenance people, support a child from the third world, collect food for the food bank, put quarters in expired parking meters."

Presenting a group of strangers with a focus that enables them to act with kindness has proven to be an excellent way to build a sense of unity and group identity. First-year college students have enthusiastically responded to this call for compassionate action, and some of these core groups formed at the Playfair program have even continued to meet as a weekly support group. Here are some of the random acts of kindness performed by core groups of first-year college students:

- Serenade the occupants of the senior citizens center.
- Sit next to someone who's eating alone in the cafeteria and strike up a conversation with him or her.
- Walk around with a Polaroid camera, take photos of groups of friends, and give the photos to them.
- Let the person behind you in line at the grocery store go ahead of you.
- Set up a free car wash in the campus parking lot.
- Get the number off a pay phone. Call the phone, and when some passerby answers, wish him a great day.
- Leave a note for the owners of a garden you pass on the way to school, letting them know how much pleasure it gives you.
- Make a meal you can bring to the homeless people in your area.
- Help the man with eighteen stray cats take care of his animals for a week.
- Volunteer as a group to work together at a battered women's shelter.

"Random Kindness" groups can meet together once, or they can continue to meet for long periods of time. At the Capistrano Valley Church of Religious Science in Orange County, California, the "Hip Hip Hooray Squad," a group of eight volunteers led by founder Bruce Snyder, has turned the concept of random acts of kindness into an ongoing celebration of reward and recognition. The 3H Squad quietly slips out of sight at large group functions and then returns dressed in brightly colored sweatshirts, playing kazoos and drawing the group's attention to unsuspecting award recipients. This Guerrilla Recognition Squad then reads a special tribute, sings a song, and leads the entire group in a chorus of "Hip Hip Hooray!" for the astonished person being celebrated.

Once a Week: Fifty-Two Ways to Have Fun on the Job

---

51 | SHARE THE PERKS

Corporate perks are a fact of life. The corner office. The rug on the floor. The executive dining room. Perks can both motivate and encourage high-quality service and serve as a reward for a job well done. But they can also serve as a painful reminder that there is a firm line dividing the corporate "haves" and "have-nots."

Martin Belanoski is the president of Metropolitan Hardware in Easton, Connecticut. On a business trip to an association meeting in Orlando, Martin had a seat in first class, while his sales manager, who traveled on the same flight, sat in coach class. As the flight progressed, Martin became more and more uncomfortable with this arrangement. He knew it was nothing personal—he was the president of the company, after all, and he always traveled first class—but that didn't make it any less

uncomfortable. So Martin walked to the back of the plane and
visited with the sales manager for a while, then returned to his
seat in the first-class cabin.

Was there anything he could do to dispel his discomfort
and the discomfort he imagined the sales manager was feeling?
He knew he would just wind up embarrassing both of them if
he tried to talk about the arrangements—their difference in
status was just a corporate fact of life. But just before the plane
landed, he had an idea. He got a bottle of champagne and a
bouquet of flowers from the first-class flight attendant and took
them off the plane with him. Then he joined the crowd of
people who were waiting for friends to come off the plane and
pretended that he was one of them. When his sales manager
came off the plane, he waved wildly to him, gave him an
enthusiastic "Welcome to Orlando!" and presented him with
the flowers and the champagne. By sharing the perks, and making light of their difference in status, he was able to cut through
the discomfort instantly. The two of them shared an upbeat taxi
ride to the hotel together, and later that evening they shared the
champagne as well.

Corporate perks may be a fact of life—but why not come
up with some novel ways to share them? How about sending
the company limo to bring a top-notch employee to and from
work one day? I'm not talking just about a manager, but about
any employee who's done a terrific job, or gone beyond the call
of duty, working late on an important project. (You can also
rent a limo for the day, if your company doesn't have one of its
own.) If budget allows, the random limo service can even become a monthly tradition in your organization, with the lucky
commuters chosen at a public ceremony at a once-a-month
lottery.

52 | CREATE YOUR OWN RITUALS FOR TRAVEL

Extended periods of business travel can cause a strain on your relationships with your family and friends. Travel time away from the office can be more fun for you, and emotionally easier for your loved ones, if you and your partner can create some rituals and celebrations around your comings and goings that can help enliven your time away from each other.

How can you remind someone who is running hysterically through the house looking for her car keys (because she is already ten minutes late for the drive to the airport) that business travel doesn't always have to be stressful? How can you stay connected to your spouse when he or she is away from home? When Playfair staff member Andy Mozenter left home for a rigorous three-week road trip, his wife Shannon wrote him a different love letter for every day that he was on the road. Every evening, in a strange hotel room in an unfamiliar city, Andy got to open a different love letter from his wife and read it just before he fell asleep.

The day your spouse is leaving on a business trip is the perfect time to give him or her some playful reminders to have some fun (and to think of you!) while he or she is away. Once he has finished packing, sneak into his suitcase, and fill pairs of socks with candy hearts. Fold love notes into her underwear. Place a photo of the two of you in his suit pocket. Write a sexy Post-it note and put it over tomorrow's entry in his business diary. Find the text of that important speech that she has been working on late at night, write her a passionate love letter, and slip it into the text, right after page three. If you're lucky, she won't discover it until she's in the middle of her presentation. And if you're really lucky, the next time she's leaving town, she'll retaliate by leaving little notes for you all around the house —under the pillow, inside the microwave, and stuck to the top of your pint of Ben and Jerry's Cherry Garcia frozen yogurt.

As important as staying connected with your spouse on the road is finding a fun way to welcome him or her home. I myself like to wear my Viking helmet, or my King Tut hat, or my Giant Safety Pin Through the Head when I pick my wife Geneen up at the airport, so she can always spot me in a crowd. The only time this backfires is when her plane is late and I need to spend an extra hour waiting.

When Luke Barber's wife Lee was away from town on an extended business trip, Luke realized that she would be returning home on Valentine's Day. So Luke called all the florists in Dallas and asked them what they did with their roses when they got too old to sell in bouquets. Many of the florists told Luke that he could have for free all the old roses he could carry away; with other florists, Luke struck a deal to buy the overage flowers at fifty cents a dozen. By Valentine's Day, Luke had collected more than twelve hundred roses.

Luke pulled the petals off all the roses and stored the rose petal collection in a large garbage bag in his refrigerator. When the big day arrived, Luke put a silk sheet on their bed and covered it with a giant heart made out of rose petals. He then bought fifty votive candles and arranged them over every available surface in their bedroom. The final touch was a path of rose petals from the front door, leading into the bedroom.

Needless to say, Lee was ecstatic to discover this extravagant Valentine homecoming.

The only difficulty, in fact, in doing something like that is . . . what do you do for an encore? The next year, just before Valentine's Day, Luke overheard Lee telling the story of the rose petals to someone on the telephone. At the conclusion of the story he heard her say, "I just can't *wait* to see what he is going to do *this* year!"

"I was stumped for a few days about how I was going to top the previous year," recalls Luke. "Soon, depression set in. I knew whatever I thought of would pale next to the previous year's gift. So, rather than even try, I just got her a dozen red roses and wrote her a card that said, 'This year for Valentine's Day I would like to spend the evening with you reminiscing about last year.' And, in fact, that's just what we did. We had so much fun. Over dinner at our favorite restaurant, I retold the whole story about how I planned it and pulled it off. We enjoyed reminiscing about it as much as we enjoyed the event itself. I think that's what makes those occasional, far-out spectaculars so wonderful—they live on in your memory for so long, and they become even more special, more joyful in the retelling."

CHAPTER 8

Having Fun in the
Difficult Times

BREAKING THE ICE

One of Playfair's core businesses is an interactive team-building
event for more than three hundred colleges and universities
in the United States and Canada. It's called "The Ultimate
Icebreaker," and it's a program to calm the new students' fears
about living in a strange, new environment, and to give them a
sense of community.

We sell the program on one very simple point. We ask our
prospective clients to consider the question, "Why do so many
first-year students drop out of college?" It's not because the
classes aren't good enough, or the professors aren't smart
enough. It's because many of the first-year students are uncomfortable socially, because they feel like they don't belong. For
many new students, college is their first time away from home;

for many others, it's their first time returning to school after years in the work force. "The Ultimate Icebreaker" program is designed to address a student's concerns and anxieties in a positive, nonthreatening forum. The program gives new students a sense of school spirit and a feeling of optimism about the future.

Every fall, there are twenty Playfair facilitators who crisscross North America, simultaneously presenting "The Ultimate Icebreaker" program at the three hundred different campuses. I travel from campus to campus, supervising as many of the programs as I can. Some weeks I feel like Bill Murray in the film *Groundhog Day:* every day I wake up in a different city, but it's always the first day of school. There is that same, excited buzz of activity, as the new students arrive. Sometimes they come alone; more often they are escorted by their parents. But always they move purposefully in a constant stream, back and forth from their automobiles to the residence halls, and back to their vehicles again. They unload their overpacked cars and move into their new lives.

After watching eight programs in six different cities during one action-packed week, I was traveling around the country in something of a daze. But on this particular afternoon, as I watched Miles Valentino present the Playfair program from an outdoor stage at Western Connecticut State University in Danbury, Connecticut, I felt instantly revived. It was a beautiful, sunny fall day, and Miles's performance was brilliant. He had the students talking to each other, laughing with one another, and cheering one another on.

Miles talked passionately to the students about the importance of living in a multicultural community. "As you look around, you'll see a lot of people who are different from you," he told them. "But the only difference you need to be concerned about is the difference you are going to make in their lives over the next four years!" The students responded with enthusiastic cheers of approval.

As soon as the program had ended, I walked over to Miles, full of praise for the way he had handled himself. We spent half an hour reviewing and fine-tuning his delivery of the program. Then we spent the rest of the afternoon enjoying the campus, walking together, and talking about our lives. As dusk began to fall, we separated, each of us on to our next campus destinations, which were hundreds of miles apart. As I drove away, I thought about the genuinely enthusiastic way the students had responded to Miles, and I felt very proud to have him as a part of the team.

The next day Miles was supposed to catch a flight to Philadelphia, and then transfer to another flight that would take him to his campus destination near Atlantic City. But Miles never made it to his next program. He took his scheduled plane as far as Philadelphia, called the college to say he wouldn't be coming, and took the next nonstop flight home to Los Angeles. The college called our New York office, concerned that the program had been canceled. We spent the next eight hours frantically trying to find out what had happened to Miles.

When Miles finally called me from his home in Los Angeles, he was very apologetic. He told me that he understood if I wanted to fire him. I reassured him that firing him was the last thing on my mind, that I was more concerned about his safety than anything else. I told him that we were all worried about him, since he had suddenly vanished from the Philadelphia airport.

In a halting voice, Miles told me that weeks before, on his very first flight of the tour, he had been on a small plane that had almost been hit by a larger plane. He had been terrified by the experience, and slowly over the following weeks he had become more and more frightened of flying. On the flight from Hartford to Philadelphia he had spent much of the time in the restroom, fighting a growing sense of terror. As soon as the plane landed in Philadelphia and he discovered that his connecting flight was on another small plane, he panicked. His nerves were shot. He knew he couldn't handle another small plane ride. So he went straight to the ticket counter and bought a ticket for the first flight back home to the West Coast.

The flight to L.A. was leaving in ten minutes, which meant he had time to call the client to say he wasn't coming, but not enough time to call the Playfair office to explain his situation. Because the client knew that Miles wasn't coming before the Playfair office knew about it, the school had canceled the program without giving us a chance to send a replacement facilitator. Miles felt very bad about that.

"But Miles," I said to him, "there's something I don't understand. We spent the whole afternoon together the day before and you never once said anything to me about being afraid of flying. There were lots of things I could have done to help you out. I could have given you the day off and had someone else do the program. I could have had you rent a car instead of flying. I could have gotten you some counseling. I could have made sure that you never had to fly on any small planes ever again. Why didn't you tell me about it?"

Miles's reply caught me completely by surprise. "If it had been anyone else but you, I would have talked about it," he said. "But you're the boss. I can't say something like that to you. I've got to look good in front of the boss."

THE ISOLATION OF THE BOSS

I was devastated by Miles's comment. I had wanted so much to create a different kind of relationship with the Playfair facilitators than the traditional employer/employee relationship. The Playfair facilitators knew I cared about them, and I knew they cared about me, too. But when push came to shove, it didn't seem to make any difference. I was still "The Boss." So much for my Great Vision about building a team.

I was despondent. "Why do I even bother to go out on the road and supervise anybody?" I asked my wife Geneen. "I'm just wasting my time. What does it matter if I coach Miles on how to do a better program, if on the important emotional issues he won't even tell me the truth? Obviously it made no difference to him if I was there or not. I came to see him during a time of crisis, and he didn't even tell me about it. It probably would have been better for Miles if I hadn't even gone to supervise him that day. I know it would have been better for me."

"That's not true," she said sympathetically. "Can you imagine how you'd be beating yourself up if you had decided not to go and then Miles had a breakdown the very next day? You'd be blaming yourself for not going, for not supporting him. I know you're disappointed in what happened, but at least this way you know the truth. At least this way you can learn something from what happened."

"Learn what?" I asked her bitterly.

"You tell me," she said softly.

I shook my head as if to say I had no answers. "Maybe I'll learn I'm in the wrong business," I replied sourly. "Maybe I'll learn that I don't know what I'm doing."

"Maybe you'll learn how to do things differently, so this won't happen again," she offered.

I shook my head again, no.

The Pain of Management

My friend Joel Goodman once told me a story that I finally understood after the incident with Miles. A sports reporter once asked Casey Stengel, one of the most successful baseball managers of all time, "What is the secret to being a great manager?" Stengel purportedly replied, "The secret to being a great manager is to keep the five guys who hate your guts away from the four who are undecided."

I realized why the Casey Stengel story always made me laugh, albeit nervously. I realized that no matter how hard I tried to make myself an equal player in the organization, the fact that I was the leader, that I had the ultimate decision-making power, would always make me different from everyone else in Playfair. In some important and fundamental way, I would always remain isolated from the rest of the group.

Even though I might have the best intentions, some of my decisions would invariably make people irritated or angry with me. Even under the best of circumstances, some of my actions would probably remind the Playfair facilitators of other supervisors they had worked for in the past. Some of their resentment toward people in positions of authority would unconsciously be sent my way. I knew that my relationship with the Playfair employees was a complex one. And while I knew our relationship would never be a terrible one, I couldn't expect it to be a perpetual love affair, either.

It was unrealistic to think that Miles—or any other employee—would confide in me, or ask for my help in times of
difficulty. They were too afraid of looking bad in my eyes. But
what was so frustrating to me was that this fear was unrealistic,
based on some stereotyped image of The Boss, not based on
any genuine understanding of who I was. If they took just a
moment to think about it, they would realize that I didn't
expect them to be perfect in their performance. They would
realize that working through painful or difficult situations together would bond us closer, not drive us farther apart.

How could I change things? The first step, I thought, was
to make the whole problem public. Miles's reaction to me as
The Boss was just that—a reaction—not any kind of thinking
response. If I could help the Playfair employees bypass the reaction stage, and instead learn to *think* about their relationship
with me, I was sure their response would be different.

My dream of establishing a strong sense of community
among the people who work for Playfair has always been my
guiding vision in running the company. If there was a solution
to be found to this problem, then we had to find the solution
together, as a community. If we were truly a team, Miles should
have felt safe in reaching out to some other members of the
group. And that hadn't happened, either.

I suddenly realized that this was about more than Miles
and his relationship with me. This was about all of us at Playfair.
This was about moving to the next level of community together.

THE NEXT LEVEL OF COMMUNITY

At the very next Playfair re-treat I asked Miles if he would be willing to stand in front of the group and tell his story. I told him that I would stand right next to him, and he agreed, though somewhat hesitantly. When the time came, we stood next to each other, facing the group, with our arms around each other's shoulders. Miles's honesty and openness in talking about how frightened he had been with each passing flight brought a hush to the room. When Miles told us how much we all meant to him, and how much he didn't want to let us down, he brought the group to tears.

What I had realized in the intervening time, I told the group, was that this wasn't just a story about Miles. This could have happened to any of us. Miles was just the first one of us to have felt the pressure of the job so strongly. "We like to pretend that we are in a glamorous profession," I told them. "And we always talk about the glamorous parts, the fun parts. But we don't take time to talk about the difficult parts, the stressful parts. You're up onstage for two hours every day, and it feels great. And sometimes, when the program goes really well, students come up to you afterward and tell you that they were moved by what you had to say, that you've made a difference in their lives.

"Of course, it feels great—for two hours. But what about the other twenty-two hours in the day? What about spending the whole day traveling? What about making small talk with total strangers all day long? What about sleeping in strange cities and strange rooms and strange beds every night? What about having hundreds or even thousands of people hanging on your every word? We do a high-pressure job, and we pretend that it's all fun and games. What happened to Miles could happen to any of us. And it *will* happen if we don't pay closer attention to how much pressure we're under."

I could tell that I had struck a chord, because the group was listening to me with rapt attention. "One thing I am very proud of is the fact that we have created an organization where everyone has jobs that are creative and challenging. I don't think anyone can say, 'I'm bored with this job.' But like everything else, there are trade-offs to be made. One of the consequences of having a job that requires you to be creative and challenged all the time is that there is no security, no formula that ensures that because things worked fine yesterday they'll work the same way today.

"Things are constantly changing all around us, all the time. Every day, you stand in front of several hundred different people who are looking to you for guidance. That means that every day you need to improvise, to think on your feet, to respond to the needs of that specific group of people. And it can take its toll on you.

"That kind of excitement, that kind of challenge is wonderful. But that kind of constant pressure can also have a negative impact on your health, if you let it. This job can wear you out if you don't take care of yourself, which is something we have never talked about."

CREATING A SUPPORT SYSTEM

Before I could begin talking about the stresses of the job, Fran Solomon jumped up and said, "I've been thinking about this for a long time. Our bodies are not designed to live like this, constantly jumping back and forth between different time zones. I notice a big difference in how I feel when I'm at home compared to how I feel when I'm on the road. This is a stressful line of work, and it's definitely taking its toll on me.

"I have a suggestion. Let's figure out how we can support each other on the road by talking about what we can do to take better care of each other. Maybe we should begin by sharing things we already do for ourselves when we're on the road."

Fran told us that she made up address labels for all the hotels where she stayed and distributed them randomly to her various friends, so everywhere she went, there were packages held for her arrival: cookies and candies and stuffed animals, and letters of support from the people she had left behind. A number of the other Playfair employees eagerly embraced this suggestion and tried it with their own friends and family.

Meanwhile, back in the Playfair home office, Nikki Jordan and Charmaine Silverstein were inspired by the idea of sending out surprise packages. They went shopping at a number of toy stores and sent out oddball gift packets and cards to their "road warriors."

Terry Sand, a facilitator based in California, has a friend named Andy Mechalecha. Everyone at Playfair knows that Terry loves the way his name sounds. Terry told the group that once in a while, whenever she had more than an hour layover in the airport, she would have her friend Andy paged, just so she could hear the operator attempt to say, *"Paging Andy Mechalecha. Andy Mechalecha to the white courtesy phone."* It always made her laugh and she suggested that we also try it whenever we felt lonely between planes.

One by one, we shared what we found difficult about life on the road and what we, as individuals, did to help ourselves. But one problem we couldn't seem to solve was the lack of connectedness we suffered while on the road. "I wish I could get a phone call from you while I was traveling," Carol Ann Fried said to me. "That would make a big difference." A number of people echoed her frustration. "Just feel the support and closeness we have right now, when we're all gathered as a group," said Janlyn Neri. "If only there were some way to take this feeling out on the road. If only I knew how to find all of you when I needed you."

There was general agreement that having access to one another would make a world of difference. But there seemed to be no way for us to keep in touch while we were all constantly in motion, crisscrossing the continent. Finally, Jordan Chouljian came up with a brilliant suggestion. "We can set up a private voice-mail system! That would link us all together on the road."

Voice mail was a never-ending series of one-way monologues, but these monologues suited the personality of our organization perfectly. By linking ourselves together electronically, we were able to carry the spirit of the re-treat out into the field with us. Whenever one of the Playfair trainers created something that would be of value to the rest of us, she could instantly share that information. Whenever one of us wanted to share our successes of the day, or ask for information, or ask for emotional support, the entire team was only a phone call away.

MILES FLIES AGAIN

One of Miles's most loyal college clients was located in a remote area of Pennsylvania. These people loved Miles so much that they had insisted if they couldn't have him as facilitator, they didn't want the program at all. To fit the school into Miles's hectic tour schedule, he would have to fly to the campus, but the nearest airport was only serviced by small aircraft. Miles had reluctantly agreed to take the flight. As I listened to my voice mail messages that day, I heard an urgent message from Miles. He had sent it out to everyone on the network: "I'm sitting in the airport in Pittsburgh and my plane leaves in half an hour. It's a small plane and I'm feeling nervous about it. But I'm going to do it. I'm going to get on that plane and I hope I'm going to be okay. Send me your support."

I felt a knot forming in my stomach. It was happening all over again. Miles needed my help and I was not about to let him down. *Please let him be okay,* I thought. Exactly thirty minutes had passed since Miles had left the message. Had he gotten on the plane? *Please let him get on the plane.* Was he in any shape to deliver the Playfair program? *Please let him be okay.*

At the heart of the voice-mail system was Jane, the computer-generated female voice, who was "on duty" twenty-four hours a day. I quickly pushed the button that connected me to Miles's mailbox. And Voice-mail Jane gave me a message I have never heard before or since. She said, "This mailbox is full. Please call back again later."

I started to panic. *His mailbox was full?* Miles was asking for help and I couldn't be there for him. I was overwhelmed by a wave of intense frustration. Miles was in trouble and the voice-mail system wasn't working. I imagined him panicking, getting on a bigger plane, and heading home again. I could think of nothing else. *And his mailbox was full.*

I dialed his number again. And again, the same message: "This mailbox is full. Please call back again later." I couldn't stand it. I pounded on the wall next to the phone booth.

Then, in my worst moment, I suddenly realized I had it all

wrong. My feelings of frustration instantly gave way to relief when I realized what had happened. It wasn't that our support system wasn't working. That wasn't it at all.

I was just too late with my message of support for Miles. *His mailbox was full because so many other Playfair staff members had beaten me to it!* They had all responded to his call for support before I had a chance to call him back. *His mailbox was full because it was full of support.* Miles had asked for support, and he had received such an overwhelming response from the Playfair community that his mailbox couldn't hold it all. It was another two days before I was actually able to get through to his mailbox, because, as Miles later explained, he had saved all the messages, and had listened to them over and over again, even after he had arrived safely at his destination.

The team was alive and well and taking care of itself. The Electronic Sangha had been born.

THE MYTH OF THE CORPORATE HERO

Most corporate cultures in this country are driven by the myth of the Corporate Hero: the person who toughs it out by himself, the person who is supercompetent in her job, the person who is ready at all times to singlehandedly save the company. Every manager operating under this system makes the same well-intentioned speech to her new employees: "If you ever need me for anything, my door is always open." And every new employee hears this speech in the same way: *"If you ever actually show up here with a problem, I'll think you don't know how to do your job!"*

Obviously, our company was no different. Unspoken in

our corporate culture was the norm that asking for help was a sign of weakness. But something important had happened over the following year. Before, Miles had been afraid to ask me for support, and he had not asked the other members of the team for help, either. And looking back, I had to admit that was understandable. There was no reason for him to think that it was safe to ask his team members for support. There was nothing in our corporate culture that rewarded him for making himself vulnerable. There was no precedent to show him that asking for support was not a sign of weakness.

But by making the issue public at our staff re-treat, we stripped the myth of the Corporate Hero of its power over us. We had taken the shame out of asking each other for help. It was clear that we had created a new norm in the organization: from this point forward it had become a mark of honor to ask for support. From this point forward each of us would feel more rewarded for being supportable than for being a Corporate Hero.

A team that is functioning as a unit is much more powerful than any single individual member of the team, more powerful even than the leader. It had always been my goal as leader for the team to be able to function without me, and now, at last, it was happening. Without the support of the team, Miles would have left the company. There was nothing that I could have done, by myself, to give him the support that he needed. But Miles's crisis had been a catalyst to move the entire organization to another level of support for one another.

This new level of support would not have been possible if not for the fun and play that had preceded it. The joy that the group had shared in the good times had prepared us to stick together through the hard times. The closeness we had built during our moments of celebration had created a firm foundation for us to stand by one another in our moments of crisis. The fact that we had laughed so well together made it possible for us to cry together.

It is easy to understand how a company that is doing well can embrace an infusion of laughter and fun and celebration into its corporate culture. It is less easy to see the place of fun and celebration during difficult times. But during the difficult times, laughter and play have their own essential purpose. In a company where the management begins to speak of "reengineering," the employees immediately think "layoffs," and morale plummets. And after the "downsizing" actually happens, many of the workers who remain suffer from survivor guilt, because so many of their friends are gone from the company. In such a difficult time, is there any reason to initiate laughter, play, celebration? Absolutely. During these difficult times it is even more important to make sure that joyfulness and celebration are still a part of our work lives.

Shared laughter in difficult times is not a sign of disrespect for the pain of the situation. Rather, it can be a first step toward healing the wounds. Shared laughter and play can reinforce the desire to rebuild a shattered team. The intentional use of laughter and play can tap into and nurture a reservoir of positive feelings, lying dormant under the surface, for the members of the team that still remain. During a time of traumatic reorganization, an infusion of positive feeling can be the platform on which to begin to rebuild the organization.

An organization cannot simultaneously mourn the past and move toward a renewed future. Shared laughter and play can inspire the survivors to remember the joyful side of working together, and can point them toward building a different kind of future, rather than remaining rooted in the past.

Serious times do not necessarily call for solemn behavior.

Solemnity as a way of life is greatly overvalued in our business culture. *Life does not become less serious when it is spiced with fun and play.* Rather, it becomes richer and more vital. It becomes less stagnant and more open to change and growth. It becomes more fully alive.

The fact that the Playfair staff responded with a sense of playfulness to a situation that involved some degree of pain showed me that we had been true to our core belief that shared laughter is a path to healing. I felt proud of the way the team reacted in a time of crisis, and I was confident that our future together would be different because of the way we had pulled together.

In the years that followed that epic re-treat, Miles became one of the most productive members of the company, traveling all over the country to conduct Playfair workshops. He began to take on more responsibility within the organization as well. He grew from a young, energetic, ball-of-fire novice, into the role of mentor to many of the younger trainers in the organization. I knew that without the support of the team, Miles would not have been able to remain with the company. I also knew that without our previous history of fun and celebration together, the team would not have been able to give both Miles and me the kind of support that carried us through our time of crisis. Things had changed. We had grown up.

The lessons the team had learned during the fun-filled times had stood us in good stead during the difficult times. I knew for certain there would be other difficult times in our future. And I felt confident that whatever those difficult times might be, we would find ways to move through them together, as a team.

• • •

Creating a corporate culture in which feelings of support, joy, and community are present every day in the workplace can be the responsibility of every person in your company, management or nonmanagement. A simple way to begin might be to follow these words based on the inspirational teachings of the Bodhisattva Samantabhadra: "We vow to bring joy to one person in the morning, and to ease the pain of one person in the afternoon. We know that the happiness of others is indeed our own happiness, and we vow to practice joy on the path of service. We know that every word, every look, every smile can bring happiness to another person. We know that if we practice wholeheartedly, then we ourselves may become an inexhaustible source of peace and joy for our clients, our customers, our coworkers, our family, and our friends."

The company that plays together stays together.

Acknowledgments

Ritch Davidson, Fran Solomon, Andy Mozenter, and Jeff Randall were there in the early days of this project and provided me with key insights, research, and support. It is no coincidence that all of them are profiled in these pages, because they live professional lives that exemplify the principles of fun at work. I am grateful that I get the chance to work with them.

Sam Kaner, Dale Larsen, and Carol Ann Fried all read the manuscript in the early stages, and I found their input to be extremely useful and thought provoking.

Angela Miller of the Miller Agency gave me coaching and editorial advice that pointed me in a most helpful direction. I am grateful for her support, sensitivity, humor, and generosity.

Luke Barber appears as a character in many of these stories; sometimes I think a whole book could be written about his exploits. In the meantime, I am thankful for his friendship and his collaboration. Someday we'll do our book together.

My thanks to Ken Blanchard, who put me together with my agent Margret McBride. Margret saw the possibilities in this book immediately, and coached me to make all the right decisions.

Laureen Connelly Rowland at Simon & Schuster is an author's dream. She is an insightful and witty editor, has a wonderful sense of the language, and is great fun to work with. She was enthused about this project from the start, and was an incredible support for me during its rush to deadline; this book is much, much stronger as a result of her work on it.

The trainers on the Playfair staff provided me with a never-ending source of pleasure; when I think of them, I feel like I have the best job in the world. I only hope I have communicated in some small way in these pages the joy and spirit that they all, without exception, bring to my life.

My assistant Charmaine Silverstein, and her assistant, Monica Perez, provided invaluable transcriptions for me at a moment's notice, which is about all I ever gave them.

Barbara Meyer, Linda Sherman, and Lori Sanchez at Admire Entertainment ran the sales and marketing side of the Playfair business without much help from me while I was finishing this book. I appreciate the depth of our relationship and the joy we have in working together.

Our cat Blanche woke up in the early hours of the morning with me, and followed me sleepily into my study, where he went through his everyday ritual of jumping on my writing desk and purring endlessly while I worked. Blanche unfortunately had his appearance edited out of this book, but he'll definitely appear in another.

And finally, my wife Geneen Roth has encouraged me for a long time to write this book, and has touched and inspired me deeply with her own beautiful writings. If it is possible for one person to be both cheerleader and muse at the same time, she has done it.

Index

We're Looking for a Few
Good Stories

If you've been **Managing to Have Fun** in your own workplace, and would like to share your stories, please send them to:

Playfair
2207 Oregon Street
Berkeley, CA 94705

Matt Weinstein and the Playfair staff are available for speeches and workshops about *Managing to Have Fun*. They can be contacted at the address above, or by phonc at (510) 540-8768; fax (510) 540-7638.